GETTING ON TOP
OF YOUR WORK

A Manual for the 21st Century Minister

Brooks R. Faulkner

Convention Press
Nashville, Tennessee

ISBN 0-7673-9457-7

Dewey Decimal Classification: 253
Subject Heading: Pastoral Work

Printed in the United States of America.

Pastor-Staff Leadership Department
LifeWay Christian Resources
of the Southern Baptist Convention
127 Ninth Avenue, North
Nashville, Tennessee 37234

Dedicated to
Shirley Anne Faulkner
my wife and partner

CONTENTS

FOREWORD

Serving as a pastor in a church is the greatest privilege anyone could ever have. It is also one of the most challenging, fulfilling, frustrating, precarious, dangerous, satisfying, and blessed vocations in the world. It is filled with contradictory, descriptive words like those above; and yet, for those who have been called of God to serve in such a capacity, it is the highest calling in the world and is compelling to those to fulfill.

One thing for sure is that the ministry is no easy calling. We have come to a time today when there is great conflict within many churches, and much of it is between the pastor and the members of the local church. As I write these lines, almost one hundred ministers per month are terminated in Southern Baptist churches. The conflicts of our culture seem to be mirrored within the fellowship of many churches.

How can a pastor serve with a sense of his high calling from God and the church and at the same time deal with the myriad of challenges that face him? How can he lead the church without being a dictator? How can he serve without becoming a doormat? How can he exhibit compassion without being indulgent and compromising? How can he hold high God's standard for personal conduct without being judgmental and harsh? How can he earn the right to be the leader for the church? How can he gain the confidence of those who have poured their lives into the church over the years and not appear to be a threat to them and to their dreams for the church?

These and many other questions make the ministry one of the most incredible opportunities and one of the most sensitive challenges to be found anywhere. Brooks Faulkner has lived in the world of the pastor with all of its challenges and obstacles for most of his ministry. He has lived in the pastor's shoes. He has faced his challenges. He has met his opposition and obstacles.

And he has given his life to communication with the pastor in a way that helps guide him through the troublesome and uncertain waters of ministry in a local church. These pages you have in your hand are born out of experience with the church and a lifelong experience with God in prayer and ministry. Brooks Faulkner knows where the pastor lives. He is acquainted with the pressures that come upon him. In these pages he has given simple, practical, and effective suggestions that will assist every pastor to become all that God desires him to be and all that he aspires to be for God. And, believe me when I tell you that Brooks Faulkner has lived out these words of counsel and has proven them in the fires of his own experience.

Let me suggest an approach to this book for you. Take it and read it through without stopping. Don't try to make notes or draw conclusions. Simply let these pages minister to you as you read through them. Then go back and study them chapter by chapter. At that time, make notes and map strategies to deal with the issues he identifies. And most of all, ask God to speak to your heart as you read and study. This book will be a valuable resource for effective ministry into the 21st century. May prayers are with you as you glean God's message for you from its pages.

James T. Draper, Jr.
President, LifeWay Christian Resources
of the Southern Baptist Convention

Introduction

When *Getting on Top of Your Work* was first released in 1973, it was released along with three other books: *Called to Joy* by Ernest Mosley, *Proclaim the Gospel* by Alton McEachern, and *Growing a Loving Church* by Robert Dale. The Pastor-Staff Leadership Department, then the Church Administration Department, was organized and functioning around the three responses to the call of God—*proclaim, lead,* and *care.* These three responses were built on a design with three interlocking circles.

Howard Foshee was the director of the Church Administration Department, and the management team was made up of Reggie McDonough, now executive director of the Baptist General Convention of Virginia; William E. Young, now retired from Lifeway Christian Resources of the Southern Baptist Convention; and Ernest E. Mosley, recently retired vice president of the Executive Committee of the Southern Baptist Convention. Other consultants at that time were Brooks R. Faulkner, Walter Bennett, Joe Hinkle, Jimmie Sheffield, James Fitch, William Halbert, Robert Dale, James Barry, Charles Treadway, and Vance Vernon. All of these men brought experience as pastors, missionaries, and church staff. All participated in developing the concepts of *proclaim, lead,* and *care* from which the four books were designed and written.

Through the past 25 years, department directors Reggie McDonough, Joe Stacker, and Don Mathis have led the Pastor-Staff

Leadership Department through many changes and developments. When Mike Miller became division director of the Church Leadership Division, he served as interim director after the retirement of Joe Stacker, and before Don Mathis began his service. During this interim Mike, along with other members of the Pastor-Staff Leadership Department, developed the new architectural design of pastoral ministries, built around *call, character,* and *competencies.*

We were preparing for the 21st century.with first-century biblical truths. With the help of Gene Mims (*Kingdom Principles for Church Growth*) and Mike Miller (*Kingdom Leadership*), the New Testament concept of *Kingdom leadership* became paramount in responding to the needs, hurts, and hopes of ministers.

The work of the minister was described in four exciting responsibilities—*leading, administering, communicating,* and *ministering.* In this context the biblical principles in Matthew 20:28 becomes vital to our understanding of the life and work of the minister: "The Son of Man did not come to be served, but to serve, and to give His life a ransom for many."

When Dr. James Draper became president in 1991, he brought with him a passion for hurting and wounded ministers. If the minister is to fulfill his work through effective leadership, administration, communication, and ministry, someone must affirm the person of the minister. Attention must be paid carefully and deliberately to the family of the minister and the team structure of the ministers who work with one another.

In 1996, at the Southern Baptist Convention in New Orleans, Dr. Draper introduced the LeaderCare team, Brooks Faulkner, Linda Miniard, Neil Knierim, Norris Smith, Barbara Harris,

Tommy Yessick, and Amy Wrye. The LeaderCare concept was built on the premise of ministering to the hurts of ministers and their families. Three action plans were prepared:

1. Prevention of major hurts and disasters in ministry through career assessments, personal and career seminars, wellness projects and seminars, resources for vocational guidance, family of minister seminars, women in church staff conferences and resources.

2. Intervention through helps with a toll-free help/care line, 1-888-789-1911; assistance for persons who have been terminated or coerced to resign in ministry, which included conflict mediation, counseling, networking through church minister relations state convention personnel, and persons who had the hurts and disappointments of ministers as a major format in their vocation.

3. Restoration—a strategy developed to help put ministers and families back on the road to a redemptive relationship with God. Included in this strategy were major steps in connecting these ministers and families with hospitals, counseling centers, state convention resources, and conference centers aimed at healing their hurts. Often helps are given to redirect the vocational energies of ministers and families. This strategy included helps to persons who were terminated for a myriad of reasons.

One thing remained central—aid and encouragement to the minister and family. From the beginning of the old *Church Administration Magazine* in 1929, through its years of lying dormant in the late thirties and early forties, and its new birth under W. L. Howse, W. O. Thomason, and Howard Foshee, *Church Administration* helped the church to be the church. The magazine was reinvented in 1956.

Pastors and staff constantly fight loneliness and isolation. It is virtually impossible to get on top of your work when you feel lonely and isolated from those who could give encouragement. This is also true for ministers' families. When pastors and staff fight the battles of difficult church members or when they fight the battles of being difficult themselves to the point of ultimatums, frequently the result is termination. Families get hurt. Children have to leave their friends. Spouses have to leave friends and jobs. It has a ripple effect that affects dozens of lives. What can be done? First, we can use the resources of our Bible. We can pray. We can seek the strength and wisdom of God. In the midst of storms and adversity, the whispers of God are hard to hear. But they are there. This book is an effort to hear those whispers. God still loves us. It just seems we are far removed from Him at times.

The outline of the original *Getting on Top of Your Work* was:

1. "Responding: The Call to be God's Leader."—Still relevant but needed a 21st-century outlook.

2. "Relating: How to Get Along with Church Members."—This is no longer enough. More later.

3. "Motivating: How to Move People."—I have learned that I know nothing about this one. Most people who try to motivate others are talking more manipulating than motivating. I think we have to find out how to help people maximize their gifts. If we help them grow, we motivate them. There is no credit for the leader in this one, just hard work.

4. "Communicating: How to Get Through to People."—Again, I found I am a novice in communicating. Communication is more sharing meaning than polishing the articulation skills.

5. "Delegating: How to Give Your Job Away."—The 21st-century cut on this is empowering, sharing the credit, helping others get a raise before you design a strategy for yourself.

6. "Deciding: How to Avoid Fence Straddling."—We changed this to "Making Time for the Important Things."

7. "Scheduling: How to Make Every Minute Count."—We think deciding and scheduling belong together.

8. "Improving: Getting It All Together."—We tried to develop this concept in three chapters: "Leaving with Grace," "Celebrating Victories," and "Waiting—It Ain't Over 'til It's Over."

GETTING IT RIGHT THE FIRST TIME

TIPS	
1	Get a good grip on your call. You are chosen.
2	Seek counsel and direction about your gifts for ministry.
3	Get all the formal academic preparation. You will need it.
4	Learn the prerequisites to licensing and ordination, and then lay out a plan for fulfilling these.
5	Include your spouse in preparation for entering ministry.
6	If you do not enjoy people, ministry will be miserable.
7	Never, ever neglect the study of God's Word.
8	Never, ever neglect the search for God's purpose through prayer.
9	Ministry is hard; but it is also fun. Remember what it is like to be a child.
10	Credibility and integrity will be get you across deep and troubling waters.
11	You cannot escape the reality of being a role model. Show your faith.
12	There will be days you will be lonely and isolated. Remember He promised never to forsake you.

God still calls. Peter spoke of the importance of the call when he said, "Therefore, brethren, be the more zealous to confirm your call and election" (2 Peter 1:10, RSV).

The best plan for our work is to get it right the first time. To do that we must respond to God's call. We must follow the model and example of the call in the Bible.

Jesus said, "Ye did not choose me, but I chose you, and

appointed you, that ye should go and bear fruit, and that your fruit should abide: that whatsoever ye shall ask of the Father in my name, he may give it you" (John 15:16, ASV).

Jeremiah was called. The "word" of the Lord came to him saying, "Arise, and go down to the potter's house, and there I will let you hear my words" (Jer. 18:2, RSV).

Moses was called. "And God said unto Moses, I AM THAT I AM: and he said, Thus shalt thou say unto the children of Israel: I AM hath sent me unto you" (Ex. 3:14, ASV).

Elijah was called, "So he went and did according unto the word of Jehovah" (1 Kings 17:5, ASV).

Paul was called. "I thank him that enabled me; even Christ Jesus our Lord, for that he counted me faithful, appointing me to his service" (1 Tim. 1:12, ASV).

I was called. I was 16. One Saturday morning my mother was sitting on the back porch shelling beans. I walked far out into the cotton patch. I felt pressure on my mind and heart. I knew something was happening, but I did not know what. I was not that close to God, but He was talking to me. Not out loud, but He was talking to me nevertheless. Between two cotton rows, I found myself on my knees in one of those pivotal, life-changing moments.

"Do you want me to preach?" I asked out loud. I knew nothing about any other kind of church vocation. The burden was not lifted immediately. I was still anxious, confused, and disturbed. But I had a sense of something being right. I walked back to the house and by my mother, still sitting on the porch.

"Momma, I think I have been called to preach." I said.

"I know," she said. She did not even look up. Years later, she told me that she had known it from the very early years of my life. I do not know how. I do not know why she never told me until that day. She knew. I did not question her credibility.

That was Saturday. Dad had gone fox hunting. He would not be back until Sunday morning. I saw him on the parking lot of

Varner River Baptist Church just before Sunday School. He came directly in from fox hunting to Sunday School.

"Dad, I think I have been called to preach."

He hugged me and cried. "I had a feeling," he said. Later he told me that the night before I was born, May 26, 1935, he prayed. "Lord, if you let him be all right, I'll do everything I can to make sure he serves you in some special way."

Have you been called? If not, find something else, quickly. Do not hesitate. Do not move past "Go." Go directly to another vocation. Being a minister is not for the timid. It is not for the weak and weary of vocational direction.

The call is not always dramatic. Sometimes it is more gradual than episodic. Those who have been called know its reality. Those who have not been called should use that uncertainty to reclaim the direction of choice. God does not gift us all the same. He does gift us. Calling into ministry is a magnificent obsession, but it is not the only way God uses persons to get His work done.

Neil Knierim says my call is a "Damascus road" experience. I used to approach discussing my call with some trepidation, fearing it might be called a spiritual *shibboleth.* But no longer. Mine is distinctive to me. Yours is distinctive to you. It may be "gradual."[1] But whether Damascus Road or gradual, it must be certain. You must know that God has called you into ministry; otherwise sooner or later you will question your purpose and direction.

When Clyde Francisco taught Old Testament prophecy, he gave us a wonderful sermon on the "call" from Isaiah 6.

Woe, the first stage of the call.—Awareness of the presence of God is a prerequisite. "'Woe to me!' I cried. 'I am ruined! For I am a man of unclean lips, and I live among a people of unclean lips, and my eyes have seen the King, the LORD Almighty'" (Isa. 6:5).

Lo, the second stage of the call.—This is the "aha" experience of responding to the question "Whom shall I send?" (Isa. 6:8).

Go, the third stage of the call.—"Go and tell this people"

(Isa. 6:9). This is our response. We *must* Go if God calls.[2]

Responding to the call, Paul wrote, "We are ambassadors for Christ, as though God were pleading through us" (2 Cor. 5:20, NKJV). "We then, as workers together with Him also plead with you not to receive the grace of God in vain" (2 Cor. 6:1, NKJV).

Reconciling Self and Others with God

"God calls his pastors and His people to this incredible 'ministry of reconciliation' as though God Himself were doing it through them (2 Cor. 5:18-19)."[3] If we are to get it right the first time, we must respond through reconciling with God. We must confess our own sins and find redemption in Christ Jesus.

That is only the beginning. We are in it for life. We must be reconcilers with God by showing others how. "But where sin abounded, grace abounded much more" (Rom. 5:20).

Dr. Draper wrote, "I found that when I neglected the priorities of soul-winning, personal devotions [we will get to that later], and genuine unselfish ministry, the work seemed to fall in around me."[4] We must spend our lives bringing others to Christ through personal soul-winning, or the well will dry up. We will find little satisfaction in anything less.

I am always surprised when persons call my name in their salvation experience. I am also always blessed. Ronnie Davis was dating Erma, a friend of my wife in Springfield, Missouri. Erma, Shirley, and I were members of College Street Baptist Church. Ronnie was not a Christian. We joined their circle of friends. Ronnie ran a bakery. He had the best cream horns in southwest Missouri. I visited his bakery frequently. I was on the staff at College Street as associate minister and custodian.

Years later we went back to College Street to participate in Ronnie's ordination as a deacon. In his testimony, he said: "When Brooks led me to Christ, I was a maverick. I cared little about the church. I am grateful for his influence." It was a small statement, but it was a monumental event in my own life.

Charles King was the son of Alvin, a deacon at New Salem Baptist Church in Bardstown, Kentucky, where I was pastor. He was just 13 when we were there. Three years ago, we went back to New Salem for a homecoming. I preached in one of my all-time favorite churches. On Saturday, we visited the parsonage. A middle-aged man walked out to our car from the church. He was accompanied by Etha Mae, his mother. Both had been making preparations for the church reunion the next day. I recognized Etha Mae but not the balding hulk of a man accompanying her.

"Brother Faulkner," he said. "You don't remember me? You played softball in that field with us. You led me to the Lord under that tree."

I remember the joy of serving Christ no more than at that moment. All the blunders, goofs, and glitches I had made in ministry were insignificant because I celebrated for a brief moment what God had called me to do—reconcile people with Christ through witnessing in His name. No greater fulfillment exists.

Getting it right means reconciling persons to Christ.

Revealing the Nature of Christ

We must reveal Christ's love and compassion. More than any other personal behavior, love and compassion best reveal one's call. Paul told Timothy, "Set an example for the believers in speech, in life, in love, in faith and in purity" (1 Tim. 4:12).

Our conduct is a model to those we serve. If we betray that model, we betray our Lord. We are in a serious business. To be careless in our morality reveals our separateness from God.

"Do not neglect your gift, which was given you through a prophetic message when the body of elders laid their hands on you" (1 Tim. 4:14). Our reflection of Christ's love and compassion is the best revelation of Christ possible outside the Scriptures. When we respond to Christ, we respond by revealing His love.

Dietrich Bonhoeffer, in *The Cost of Discipleship*, said we are "set apart" to reveal the love and compassion of Christ. He called this "sanctification." Sanctification has three aspects:

1. "Holy living will be achieved only by not being conformed to the world."
2. "Christian living will be the result of walking with Christ."
3. "Their sanctification will be hidden, and they must wait for the day of Jesus Christ."[5]

The third aspect is most interesting and, perhaps, confusing. We are to avoid calling attention to ourselves as ones who reveal Christ's love and compassion. We are not to exploit our position as ministers. We must not set ourselves *up* as spiritual models; rather we are to set ourselves *apart* to do the work of ministry hidden from the accolades of others, thus "hidden and waiting for the day of Jesus Christ." This is a scathing judgment on those who take pride in their humility. Those who call attention to themselves as ambassadors of the love and compassion of Christ negate their effectiveness. True ambassadors have nothing to prove except the love of Christ. This is a hard task. It is easier to function with widespread appreciation and approval. It is difficult to serve and function in the "out of the way" places of ministry where appreciation and approval are difficult, and often impossible, to find.

Responding Through Recovering from Adversity

What one thing, more than any other, picks us up when we are down? Our call. We reach back to the time when God placed us in His purposive kingdom plan by setting us aside.

Ministers are vulnerable. We are exposed in our leadership. Some people enjoy taking potshots at us. Don Mathis wrote a marvelous article, "What to Do as a Pastor when People Hate Your Guts."[6] Knowing that someone doesn't like us is disturbing, but it is part of the job.

We are different. Some church members see us so different they are intimidated. If they aspire to leadership, they may become competitive. We know we are only different in the sense that we have distinctive tasks to do for God. They often see us as being different in the sense of thinking we are morally better than they. They see us representing God in public worship and organizational meetings. It is natural for them to want to bring us down. It is not that they are vicious and vindictive persons (though some may be); it is just a normal response to an imposing situation.

Our call confirms our ability to recover from adversity. I preached from Hebrews 11, the "Roll Call of Faith," for years before I finally recognized the impact of verse 39. "These were all commended for their faith, yet none of them received what had been promised" (Heb. 11:39). God did not promise the minister financial prosperity. Those fly-by-night con artists who try to convince millions of their need for money by promising financial prosperity are deceitful and unscriptural. The promise of better things in this life does not always consist of financial rewards. But there is a promise: "God had planned something better for us" (Heb. 11:40). It may not be (and in most cases, is not) in this life, but He has planned something better for us.

I take great comfort in that verse. I try to reach back to the time when I was 16 years old and remember what God has planned for me. I then remember the promise that He has something better planned, and 98 percent of the time I overcome. I have had a few times when I succumbed to the adversities. I have had a few times when remembering my call did not help me recover from my despair, but most of the time, yes.

Joe McKeever interviewed six pastors about what they consider unique ministerial pressures.[7] To preface their interviews, he claimed, "These men love the ministry, are devoted to the church, have a strong sense of God's call upon their lives, and would not want to be in any other line of work. None of them came to me with a gripe, I drew it out of them."

One man said: "No one understands the pastor's job except he, himself. But, everyone thinks they do. So everybody is an expert. We get criticized as any leader does, but we don't have the liberty to react to it the way other people would. . . . As a rule, we cannot even respond. If we do, it has to be done with gentleness and kindness. Once in a while you'd like to 'vent' with complete abandon."

Some pastors have large storage bins of anger. These storage bins need dumping. Ministers can find many ways to recover from adversity. We do not have the luxury of exploding to release the pressure. We must find more acceptable, constructive measures. One way to recover from adversity is to reach back for the basics. Reach back to the time when God called us into ministry. We must reach back to that event (either "Damascus road" or "gradual") and find the ingredients for recovery from adversity. At that moment we realize we "got it right the first time."

Paul admonished the Galatians, "Let us not become weary in doing good" (Gal. 6:9). Roy Moody, director of evangelism, Kansas-Nebraska Baptist Convention suggested: "It is obvious Paul had never pastored a Baptist church. He was a denominational worker giving advice to pastors." I resent that, but I don't deny it. He was probably right. Adversity is part of the job. Recovering from adversity is a forgone conclusion. It is tough. It is not impossible. It is just tough.

---

[1] Neil Knierim and Yvonne Burrage, *God's Call: The Cornerstone of Effective Ministry* (Nashville: Convention Press, 1997), 8.

[2] Clyde T. Francisco, in a 1960 lecture, Southern Baptist Theological Seminary, Louisville, Kentucky.

[3] Henry Blackaby and Henry Brandt, *The Power of the Call* (Nashville: Broadman & Holman, 1997), 57.

[4] James T. Draper, in a personal memo to Brooks Faulkner, 1 September 1998.

[5] Dietrich Bonhoeffer, *The Cost of Discipleship*, rev. ed., trans. R. H. Fuller (New York: Macmillan, 1960), 252.

[6] Don Mathis, "What to Do as a Pastor When People Hate Your Guts," *Growing Churches*, Fall 1999.

[7] Joe McKeever, guest editorial, *Baptist Message*, 27 August 1998: 4.

ANTICIPATING THE WORST; PLANNING THE BEST

TIPS	
1	Every answer for every difficult question is in God's Word, but sometimes our anxiety makes it hard to find.
2	If everything were going well, your church probably wouldn't need you.
3	Don't stir the pot if you can't wait for the beans to cook, or don't leave the stove on if you are going to a "better opportunity."
4	Bad things happen to good ministers.
5	God can use bad things to bring about His kingdom.
6	One bad game does not mean the season is over.
7	Preparation is hard work, but it's worth it.
8	There is no substitute for common sense when decision making is hard.
9	If you have to punt and the punt is blocked, share the responsibility.
10	Bear Bryant would forgive anyone who gave his best. So will God.
11	Show faith and do daily reality checks. Balance will help you survive.
12	If the weight-challenged woman has sung and you lose, the best medicine is getting prepared for next week.
13	The early bird gets the worm, but the second mouse gets the cheese. Anticipate the worst, but plan for the best.
14	He who hesitates is probably right.

"All Scripture is God-breathed and is useful for teaching, rebuking, correcting and training in righteousness, so that the man of God may be thoroughly equipped for every good work" (2 Tim. 3:16-17).

The first lesson in preparing is to get baptized in the Scriptures. Study them. Remember them. Apply them. Get comfortable with them. This is the best way to get prepared for the things to come. And things will come. The good times—they will come. But the bad times—they will come, too. The key words in preparation are *thoroughly equipped*. Anticipate.

Tommy Yessick, a member of our LeaderCare team, was a manager of Bear Bryant's Alabama Crimson Tide Football team from 1968 to 1972. Recently, I asked him what was the number one leadership lesson he learned from Bear Bryant. Without blinking an eye, he said, "Anticipate details."

Of all the leaders in the history of American football lore, Bear Bryant was one of the most—if not *the* most—legendary. He was "thoroughly equipped." The reason, according to Dr. Yessick (now a wellness expert), was that he anticipated details. He prepared for the worst. If things went terribly wrong, he had a plan. If he was one touchdown behind, he had a plan. If he was two touchdowns ahead, he had a plan. He even implemented some plays that would be used only once in a season. He knew he was being scouted by future opponents, so he would implement a play just to have them spend time preparing for it. Then he would not use the play. He would anticipate the opponent's using energies to prepare for options he might never use.

Tommy recalls one amusing story about an equipment manager's faux pas. He forgot to take the footballs to the game. We are talking about major panic. How can a football team practice without a football? Fortunately, they called a state patrolman in Tuscaloosa; and with sirens blasting, the footballs arrived, although late. Then the real anxiety began. How do you keep this information from Bear Bryant? Night footballs from trunks and equipment bags were used until the others arrived. A major campaign was planned to keep the amused players from spilling the beans. Here the king of anticipation was being asked to believe that nothing out of the ordinary was going on while old, borrowed footballs were being tossed around the practice field. Tommy does not know if Bear Bryant knew what happened. Poor Allen Edwards will live on in infamy in the legends of Bear Bryant.

The metaphor becomes even more vivid for the minister. How can the minister anticipate details without the help and guidance of the Scriptures? The Bible helps us prepare for every unanticipated surprise and/or adversity. Becoming serious students of the Scriptures is vital to our survival.

Much can be said for the beginning of 1 Timothy 2: "I urge, then, first of all, that requests, prayers, intercession and thanksgiving be made for everyone—for kings and all those in authority, that we may live peaceful and quiet lives in all godliness and holiness. This is good and pleases God our Savior, who wants all men to be saved and to come to a knowledge of the truth" (vv. 1-4).

In the theme of "comfort, comfort my people," Isaiah 40:3, suggests, "A voice of one calling: 'In the desert prepare the way for the LORD; make straight in the wilderness a highway for our God." In the 1950s, under the presidency of Dwight Eisenhower, the United States began a major construction effort to build a national interstate highway system. Today the minister must prepare for the way of the Lord by creating a new information superhighway. He must know how to connect the biblical truths with the day-to-day activities of living. It is mandatory that we make the Bible relevant to the contemporary events of life.

God's Call Is Our Reality Check

It is hard at times. It is almost always meaningful. Ministry is the "it." God's call is our reality check to the "it."

Sometimes pastors feel they can't believe they get paid for doing what they love to do. *Calling Church and Seminary into the 21st Century* by Donald E. Messer, president of the Iliff School of Theology in Denver, Colorado, gave some poetic and powerful language about this call in the sketch of a portrait of a pastor in comparison and relationship with other professions. Messer credits Bob and Polly Holmes for the imagery,

> I'm not a physician, but I've stood at many a bedside when a life hung in the balance. I'm not an attorney, but I've sat in court through many an anxious trial. I'm not a law-enforcement officer, and yet I have been on the scene—all the way from barroom to jail, from second-floor flat to state reform school, reaching for people who need desperately to be reached and understood and helped. I'm not a judge nor an FBI agent nor a psychiatrist, and yet my job is to try to bring justice to bear on injustice, truth on falsehood, and love on hate.[1]

Our call brings us back to the reality of our task. It prepares us for details which are difficult, but not impossible, to anticipate.

Moses knew the importance of reaching back for his call as a reality check. He said, "If your Presence does not go with us, do not send us up from here. How will anyone know that you are pleased with me and with your people unless you go with us? What else will distinguish me and your people from all the other people on the face of the earth?" (Ex. 33:15-16).

How will our people know that we are called of God unless we give evidence of that call? We must tell them about our call. We must remind them that God has given us a mission. We must be about our Father's business as was Jesus. We must pave the way with the model of Christ. We cannot lead people unless we give constant evidence of the call of God. We cannot maintain contact with the mission and purpose of God unless we maintain contact with the commission of God by our call. Knierim reminds us in his book, *God's Call: The Cornerstone of Effective Ministry*, that Moses sought the presence of God before he tried to lead.[2]

God's Book Is Full of Answers

After Abraham was put to the test, God intervened. Isaac, his only son, was offered as a sacrifice. When things are at their worst, God is at His best. So God intervened with the sacrificial lamb. He provided. Could there have been a more demanding test? Abraham was willing to give his only son. That is worse than losing your church. That is worse than facing a critical onslaught by the deacons. It is worse than cancer. It is worse than having your credit card reach the max, and a child must have braces. God provided. In fact, Abraham named the place Jahweh Jireh, "The LORD will provide" (Gen. 22:14).

In preparation, the best resource is the Bible. When anticipating the details of the unknown, the Bible has many answers.

It is also the most taken for granted. Ministers spend a lot of time with the Bible. They prepare to preach and to teach. They prepare devotionals. They use the Bible for many things. But the Bible is used best as a personal road map. When Dr. Draper and I were discussing the beginning of this book, he said: "Be sure you spend time on the priorities in ministry. I found low points in my ministry occurred when I did not spend the appropriate amount of time in personal devotions with God's Word."

James McCutcheon began his work on *The Pastoral Ministry* with "The Parish Minister's Professional Devotional Life." It was the very first chapter.[3] He suggested that Jesus was the model for this devotional time. The Bible taught that He found a place where He was not likely to be disturbed. "In the morning, a great while before day, he rose and went out to a lonely place, and there he prayed" (Mark 1:35, RSV).

The Bible is the best resource for this devotional detour from the stress and loneliness of ministry. The Bible gives comfort. "I am in pain and distress; may your salvation, O God, protect me" (Ps. 69:29). And it does.

But there is a glitch. Some questions seem to have no answers. I do not understand the dismal, decaying distress of manic depression. I have known ministers who were married to persons with this illness. I have known ministers who suffered from this disorder. It is devastating. We know that the Bible promises, "But God is the strength of my heart and my portion forever" (Ps. 73:26). But sometimes it seems so far away. The comfort we seek feels at arm's length. It is close but not completely captured. During these times the struggle must be determined. We must doggedly dig out the undercurrents of hope when things seem most hopeless.

I do not understand the senselessness of random violence. I am appalled at the thought of two young boys taking the lives of a teacher and five children. I am confused with the suicide of a daughter of a minister who has been a model servant of God. I am disturbed by the thought of a deacon physically attacking his pastor because of a disagreement over the 5-percent raise in the salary of a staff member in the church.

When we read the words, "The words of a gossip are like choice morsels; they go down to a man's inmost parts," we search for the balm of God's words. We find this balm just one sentence away. "The name of the LORD is a strong tower; the righteous run to it and are safe" (Prov. 18:8, 10). But when the pain is so vivid, the words are faint. When the bleeding is visual from a daughter who is about to lose her friends because of her father's termination from the church, it is difficult to reach back and find the comfort of God's words. Nevertheless, they are there. God's Word is our safety net from the anticipated details of working with persons who confuse us. When we are preparing to be God's servants, nothing prepares us as thoroughly as God's Holy Word in the Scriptures.

On Thursday, January 22, 1998, America Online carried a series of one-liners. Some were amusing. Others were amusing and painful. I believe the term is *bittersweet*. Two of the one-liners apply to this discussion of preparing by anticipating details with the encouragement of God's Word. "If everything seems to be going well, you have obviously overlooked something." Where did we get the idea that everything is supposed to go well in ministry? We would not need God's Word if everything were going well. But we do need God's Word. And everything doesn't go well. As a matter of fact, if everything were going well, why would churches need ministers, anyway?

A second one-liner was, "If you ain't makin' waves, you ain't kickin' hard enough!" The grammar is bad. The truth is prophetic. God expects us to make waves. He expects us to unsettle the settled. And when we do our job, why should we be surprised that people to whom we minister are upset? Certainly we need God's Word to anticipate details. The details are that we are going to have adversity, but God is going to comfort us with His Holy Word.

Learning Is a Never-Ending Story

"So that the man of God may be thoroughly equipped for every good work" (2 Tim. 3:17). Learning is a never-ending story. I love the phrase *lifelong learner.* Howard Foshee, the department director of the Church Administration Department in the fifties and sixties, was fond of saying, "The theme of the military was 'train, retrain, retrain, retrain, or die.'" It is true of the military. It is true for the minister. Every day we learn something. Often, the thing we learn is how little we know.

The best selling book, *Jesus CEO* by Laurie Beth Jones has a chapter entitled, "He Had a Plan." In the first paragraph, she writes, "A franchising consultant once told me, 'A good idea is worth one dollar. The plan for implementing that idea is worth a million dollars.'"[4]

We learn the plan in a formal education. Every minister, regardless of age, should start with that formal education. High school, college, and seminary are prerequisites to preparing. A part of the lifelong learning process is to continue that formal education. Colleges and seminaries have developed a plan for continued learning for any minister. Whether in a formal degree program or a diploma program, the preparation is vital to effectiveness and accountability.

But it does not stop there. The million-dollar value is implementation. That process is a never-ending story. We learn from God's Word. We learn from personal devotions. We learn from our family. We learn from our church. We learn from our friends. We learn from deacons, teachers, staff persons. We "train, retrain, retrain, retrain, or die."

We learn from our mistakes. Mark Twain is often credited with the phrase, "There is nothing new under the sun, except the history we missed." Harry Truman quoted that statement on several occasions. So a part of preparing, or anticipating, details is studying the history of our mistakes. We learn from them.

Jones added, "What good does it do to stir up a crowd if you do not give them a constructive outlet for their energy?"[5] If we are to continue to anticipate the details, we must continue to learn. That is hard work. It is easier to stir up a recipe than to gather the ingredients and cook the meal.

The never-ending story of learning must ultimately be guided by our heart. There is no substitute for good, common horse sense. The Holy Spirit works best in giving us good common sense in critical situations. The key is to permit the function. A part of the "Experiencing God" phenomenon is to find what God is doing and what God wants and do it with Him. Learning which anticipates the details in ministry is giving God room to work. His Holy Spirit will be operative if we can get past our own selfish wants and needs. "There is a way that seems right to a man, but in the end it leads to death" (Prov. 16:25). But just a few words before that oft-quoted passage are the words, "The wise in heart are called discerning, and pleasant words promote instruction. Understanding is a fountain of life to those who have it, but folly brings punishment to fools. A wise man's heart guides his mouth, and his lips promote instruction" (Prov. 16:21-23). We must learn to work with good, common horse sense guided by God's Holy Spirit if we are to continue to learn.

If Everything's Coming Your Way, You May Be in the Wrong Lane

"Ministers are in touch with 'the most important happenings of people's lives' and 'on the inside of the deepest struggles in their experiences.'"[6] And if not, they are in the wrong lane. If everything is easy, it could be boring.

As I write this chapter, it is September 9, 1998. Last night a historic event took place. Millions of baseball fans around the world watched Mark McGwire hit his 62nd home run, surpassing Roger Maris' home run record of 61. The line drive over the left-field fence looked easy for him. The massive arms, the large frame, and the sense of deliberate concentration made him appear to have the bull by the horns, the world on a string, and all the other cliches imaginable.

Metaphorically, all of us have watched ministers who seem to have everything they touch turn to gold. Their churches grow. Their staffs continue to multiply. They are selected for significant committees and denominational posts that are the envy of their peers. They are personable. They are attractive. They just seem to be sitting on a rainbow.

But we have also had the experience of knowing some of these ministers up close and personal. Their struggles are real. Their aspirations have been dampened. They have made mistakes. Some of their families are disarrayed and dysfunctional. One pastor gave us a transparent look into his personal life: "You have the same spiritual struggles as the next person. Unfortunately, you have no latitude, no time, no liberty to deal with them, because next Sunday you will be standing behind the pulpit proclaiming the unsearchable riches. Sorry, friend, no mid-life crisis allowed here. Try telling the deacon chairman, 'I won't be at the meeting this afternoon. I'm too depressed.' So the pastor tries his best to handle it through prayer and faith and work, when what he may need is rest and quietness and a counselor."[7]

Mark McGwire had years of practice and hard work preparing to break the home-run record. He took care of his mind and body. He listened carefully to instructors and coaches. He learned from everyone around him. He said in the post-game interview: "Only Sammy Sosa [seated by him in the interview, the Chicago Cubs outfielder who the night before had hit 58 home runs and was also in the home-run record chase] knows the pressure that has gone into the summer. I am glad it is over." If everything seems to be coming your way, it is true that you may be in the wrong lane.

Therefore, in getting on top of your work, prepare by anticipating details. Play out the scenes as best you can, and then depend on the Holy Spirit for guidance.

God's call is our reality check. Go back to the call again and again. God's Book is full of answers. It creates questions as well, but most answers are there. Continue to learn by training, retraining, and retraining. And finally recognize the reality that if everything is coming your way, you may be in the wrong lane.

---

[1] Donald E. Messer, *Calling Church and Seminary into the 21st Century* (Nashville: Abingdon, 1995), 31.

[2] Neil Knierim and Yvonne Burrage, *God's Call: The Cornerstone of Effective Ministry* (Nashville: Convention, 1997), 47.

[3] James McCutcheon, *The Pastoral Ministry* (Nashville: Abingdon, 1978), 11ff.

[4] Laurie Beth Jones, *Jesus CEO* (New York: Hyperion, 1996), 87.

[5] Ibid., 87–88.

[6] Messer, 31.

[7] Joe McKeever, guest editorial, *Baptist Message*, 27 August 1998: 4.

GETTING ALONG WITH DIFFICULT PERSONS

TIPS	
1	The most difficult part of the minister's job is loving difficult people.
2	Be kind to difficult people; you never know what demons they are fighting.
3	Friends may come and go, but enemies accumulate. Don't rush to judgment.
4	Church rage is a lot like road rage, except the weapons are words instead of automobiles.
5	Arguing is the beginning of a long journey into futility.
6	The best way to deal with a person who wants the upper hand is to extend the hand of fellowship.
7	You cannot be manipulated by difficult persons without giving them permission to do so.
8	A reconciliation always begins with someone willing to give another the benefit of the doubt.
9	Almost any relationship can be improved if we recognize the fact that we cannot change persons. Only God can do that.
10	It is better to lose with grace than win with arrogance.
11	It is easy to avoid criticism—simply do, say, and be nothing.
12	Life is full of absurdities; difficult people try to make sense out of all of them.

Mistakes are springboards to personal growth; only the difficult person sees mistakes as ends in themselves.	13
For every action, there is an equal and opposite reaction. Some are far worse than others.	14
The two most distinguishing traits of a difficult person are hopelessness and helplessness. Point them toward hope and help, and you have made a friend forever.	15
A meeting that lasts over an hour is a breeding ground for difficult people.	16
The same energy that makes one difficult can be channeled into creativity if plugged into the right outlet.	17
The Bible is a book of solutions to difficult persons, but the application is often like surgery without an anesthetic.	18
Difficult persons enjoy the comfort of anonymity, resulting in unsigned letters and craftily shaped rumors. Throw away the anonymous letters. Tell the truth, and you will not have to remember what you said.	19
Difficult people have lost sight of the fact that adversity is the breeding ground for possibilities and opportunities. Your job is to help them see.	20
You can't reason with prejudiced people. They did not get prejudiced by reason but by the lack of it.	21
Jesus said, "Be ye kind." Did He know about us?	22

We're tempted to generalize about difficult persons. An easy generalization is to say *the* most difficult are those who feel they are never wrong. A popular psychiatrist and best-selling author of the '70s wrote: "The poor in spirit do not commit evil. Evil is not committed by people who feel uncertain about their righteousness, who question their own motives, who worry about betraying themselves. The evil of this world is committed by the spiritual fat cats, by the Pharisees of our own day, the self-righteous who think they are without sin because they are unwilling to suffer the discomfort of significant self examination."[1]

The most difficult part of a minister's job is loving people like those. Loving the contrite is not difficult; they are approachable. Loving the guilty is not difficult; they are searching for relief, and you represent the possibility of relief. Loving the lonely or desperate or hurt is not difficult; they are reaching for hope, and you may be their ambassador of hope. But loving those who are never wrong *is* difficult. It is difficult to love those who "have the best interests of the church at heart" and, at the same time, feel that you do not. These people are faithful, but faithfully irritating. They are dedicated, but dutifully dedicated to guiding and correcting the wrongs. They are predictable and consistent, but so much so that they rob themselves and others of spontaneity and fun in life. They are difficult.

Church members are not the only difficult people. Frequently, the ministers who work with us are difficult. On more than one occasion, I heard Howard Foshee say, "Show me a church-staff person who is unhappy in his or her work, and I will show you a person who wants someone else's job."

On first glimpse, that statement feels a little too all encompassing. Admittedly, it has some leaks. But the more I have worked with pastors and staff, the more wisdom I see in it. Some staff persons feel they would do a better job of pastoring than the pastor. Unfortunately, they share this conviction with significant decision makers in the church. The problem begins when these decision makers are persuaded by the staff person. Some pastors feel they would like to go to another church, a larger opportunity; but that church already has a pastor, so unhappy pastors and staff become unhappy because they want someone else's job.

Pastors and staff can take comfort in the words of Proverbs: "The LORD detests all the proud of heart. Be sure of this: They will not go unpunished" (Prov. 16:5). But the privilege of punishment is not ours, nor will we always see the punishment. Punishment is reserved for the Lord. We may be tempted to say, "Lord, just let me get a glimpse. That's all I ask. I don't want him to break his ankle, just sprain it. Then I will know him by his limp."

Difficult persons have long-lasting effects. "A happy heart makes the face cheerful, but heartache crushes the spirit" (Prov. 15:13). A highly personal, critical, anonymous note can be devastating. The family you ministered to during the suicide of a teenage son can no longer stand the pain of seeing the people associated with their crisis. They move their membership. The minister takes it personally. They are not intentionally difficult, but their actions hurt the minister. How can these persons be so ungrateful? But ingratitude is not even a part of the puzzle.

In the long run, dealing with difficult people takes a toll. It tears at the spirit. It creates unhappy work relations. It contributes to depression and, often, desperation. Difficult persons are hard to love. Difficult persons often seem impossible. But the reality is *we have to work with difficult persons if we are called into ministry. It is part of our job. It is what God expects.* This part of *Getting on Top of Your Work* is designed to give some ingredients for doing just that.

Jesus was always being tested. An expert in the law came to Him with the question, "Teacher, which is the greatest commandment in the Law?" They wanted Him to comment in order to bring charges of blasphemy against Him. They knew they could bring legal charges if they could bring blasphemy (*giddupha*) charges because "in the Biblical context, blasphemy is an attitude of disrespect that finds expression in an act directed against the character of God." [2]

Jesus was quick to respond. He did not dodge the issue. "Love the Lord your God with all your heart and with all your soul and with all your mind" (Matt. 22:37). It takes a strong heart, soul, and mind to love God, but the hardest part was yet to come. "This is the first and greatest commandment. And the second is like it: 'Love your neighbor as yourself.' All the Law and the Prophets hang on these two commandments" (vv. 38-40). He knew He was talking with an expert lawyer. He knew the question was loaded. Yet He did not hedge. "All the Law and the Prophets hang on these two commandments." A part of the responsibility of getting on top of your work is to learn to love the unlovely. Our vindictive nature must take a backseat to our primary responsibility.

You cannot love difficult persons without being healthy yourself. The Menninger Foundation has drawn up a list of traits necessary for emotional maturity. They are:

- The ability to deal constructively with reality.
- The capacity to adapt to change.
- A relative freedom from symptoms that are produced by tensions and anxieties.
- The capacity to find more satisfaction in giving than receiving.
- The capacity to relate to other people in a consistent manner with mutual satisfaction and helpfulness.
- The capacity to sublimate, to direct one's instinctive, hostile energy into creative and constructive outlets.
- The capacity to love.[3]

The ability to love difficult and/or unruly persons in a church requires a healthy person who has tasted of God's grace. Jesus' message was strong and clear: If you really want to know what God's law is to humankind, you must know how to love. Because God is love.

I am going to use six of the classic patterns of personality to consider difficult persons and how to get along with them. But first a disclaimer. I find myself in each of these. I find myself difficult in dealing with many people. I find myself exceptionally difficult in dealing with specific persons. In other words, this is not an accusation. This is not a judgment. This is an effort to keep the second portion of the greatest commandment that Jesus gave us.

Each of us has distinctive traits that cause us to behave "distinctively." It simply means adjustments are necessary on our part and on the part of those who work with us. This often means we become difficult to others. Therefore, let us begin by admitting that there is some of the "difficult" in all of us. That does not mean we are impossible but rather simply difficult.

The six difficult behavior patterns we will discuss are:
1. The Overly Suspicious Person
2. The Circumferential Person
3. The Histrionic Person
4. The Star Performer
5. The Passive-Aggressive Person
6. The Borderline Personality-type Person

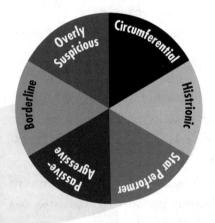

In addition to the above disclaimer, some characteristics are necessary in developing a loving attitude. Developing these characteristics is not easy. It is, however, possible. Let's consider these.

Getting Prepared to Love the Difficult Person

Remember your call.—Refresh your memory daily. God has called you to a task. It includes loving people who are hard to love.

Control your temper.—"So from now on we regard no one from a worldly point of view" (2 Cor. 5:16). The minister does not have the luxury of unbridled candor. No value can be added by saying everything you feel. The control of the tongue is a major factor in getting along with church members and/or church staff who display difficult characteristics. There is arguably some therapeutic value in venting or dumping the negative loads. But controlling your temper means learning where and when to vent or dump. Your goal should never be deliberately to embarrass the person, even if that person is deliberately trying to embarrass you.

Be quick to forgive and even quicker to ask forgiveness.— Jesus had the most difficulty with the self-righteous. Self-righteous persons have a gift for leaving a bloody trail of disorder. They are hard to forgive. But the worst is yet to come. They are even harder to ask for forgiveness. When a gentle person is offended by our thoughtlessness, we can comfortably ask for forgiveness. When a self-righteous and "always right" person is offended by our thoughtlessness, "I was wrong; please forgive me" gets stuck in our throat. This is a good time to remember Jesus' words, "For everyone who exalts himself will be humbled, and he who humbles himself will be exalted" (Luke 14:11).

The echoes of imagination play tricks on us. We do not like to hear the words, *I told you so.* We are reluctant to play into the hands of those who enjoy one-upmanship. As a result, we are cautious about admitting the need for forgiveness. We are even more cautious about asking for forgiveness. But having egg on your face is not the worst thing that could happen. Eggs represent the first meal of the day. The day is young. There are other meals.

My dad had a theory about self-righteous persons. He felt they did not think very highly of themselves. The idea of being right was simply important because in their minds it elevated them a little higher than their neighbor. He said that relating to self-righteous people is a lot like breaking a wild horse. The first thing you have to do is give them enough rope to feel some freedom. A wild horse does not want to feel everything has been taken away. It doesn't hurt to say, "You could be right." It isn't the end of the world to say, "I could be wrong." If you are gentle with a wild horse, you will have a friend for life. If you put the bits on too tight or too quick, someone will get hurt.

Don't resent the person who is full of bitterness.—Almost all get over it. Additionally, most of the time we do not know what they are really bitter about. The primary complaint of a bitter person is almost always secondary.

In the movie *The Apostle,* Robert Duvall—who starred in it, wrote, directed, and produced it—included a scene in which a man came to the small Louisiana church to challenge the preacher. He stood outside the church and insulted the preacher, ultimately provoking him into a fight. Billy Bob Thornton played the small part of the prejudiced and miserable challenger. When the preacher/apostle placed a Bible before him, the challenger was brought to his knees and to a saving knowledge of Jesus Christ. If the apostle, a Holiness preacher drawn from real life, had wilted to the pleas of his members to call the sheriff, the bitter man would not have been saved.

Don't resent bitter people. Even though you are the primary target, you are most often a secondary conflict.

Write down the five areas where you are the most stubborn, and see if you can soften them.—I did this exercise for myself. It looked like this: (1) anonymous critical letters, (2) political gurus, (3) intolerant authority figures, (4) Vanderbilt football critics, and (5) holier-than-thou preachers.

I noticed that even in my list, I was stubborn. I try to reach back for the wise counsel of Proverbs 16:21, "The wise in heart are called discerning, and pleasant words promote instruction."

Remember that everything has God's fingerprints on it.— How could Jesus' disciples have known what was in store? Judas was disenchanted to the point of betrayal. Peter objected vehemently but later fizzled. All resisted the process, yet it was God's plan for redemption. Grace is more powerful than logic. Job responded to his critic: "Though one wished to dispute with him

[God], he could not answer him one time out of a thousand. His wisdom is profound, his power is vast. Who has resisted him and come out unscathed? He moves mountains without their knowing it" (Job 9:3-5). We cannot know what God has in store for us. How can we know how He will use difficult persons to gain His ultimate, purposive will? Only in reflection can we see God's fingerprints. We cannot see His hand when it is moving. We have to have faith to discover the fingerprints of God.

Learn to live with ambiguity.—Change is a certainty. Change is uncomfortable. It is also exciting. Working with difficult persons gives room for a lot of ambiguity. Little certainty can be established. Even when it is glimpsed, it is in motion. People rarely know why they are difficult. It is as ambiguous to them as it is to those who are trying to relate to them.

We must live with the commas of life. There are few periods. We waste our energy in trying to determine why people act the way they do. How can we know if they do not know?

Perhaps many arguments could be settled if we would learn to live without that expression, "I'm just trying to understand." Marriages could be saved if partners would spend less energy in trying to understand the confusing behavior of the other partner. As a matter of fact, the mystery of many relationships is maintained because one does not completely understand the behavior of the partner. Understanding is pleasant—not mandatory.

Pastors and staff could stay longer in churches if they could live with ambiguity. No one knows why churches act as they do. No one understands completely why some persons behave predictably and others do not. But ambiguity is reality.

The Overly Suspicious Person

Eliphaz, Bildad, Zophar, and later Elihu, came to "comfort" Job (2:11). Perhaps they wanted to see him squirm. The discourses they gave him were not all that comforting.

"Does God pervert justice? Does the Almighty pervert what is right?" (Job 8:3). The implication is, What have you done wrong? What is your sin? The overly suspicious person is the first one to a gruesome automobile wreck. The overly suspicious person is the first one to give pseudo-comfort in the name of friendship in order to gather the sordid details. If he can gather them quickly, he can be the first to dispense them to broader audiences.

The overly suspicious watch the grief at a funeral. The real friends are those who give comfort one month, six months, one year later, when the shock wears off and needed comfort is self-evident. The overly suspicious are more curious than compassionate.

A pastor buckles under the load. He ends up in a fetal position in his office. A staff member helps get him home and later to the hospital. He makes arrangements for his workload of visitation, pulpit supply, counseling, and other administrative responsibilities. He cares for his family. He sees that food is provided during the first few days of crisis. At the same time, a second staff member laments to one of the administrative support persons: "He's the last person on earth I would have expected this to happen to. He is always showing us how to deal with stress, and now this. I wonder what the real story is." We can call this second staff person Bildad. The first staff person acted a lot like Jesus.

The classic text of therapists is *Disorders of Personality DSM-IV and Beyond* by Theodore Millon with Roger D. Davis. In this account the characteristics of the suspicious person are described:

- Envy and jealousy exhibited by vigilant mistrust.
- Provocative interpersonal behavior accompanied by irritability.
- "Grimly resistant to sources of external influence and control."
- "Embellishes trivial achievements in line with semi-grandiose self-image."
- "Reveals tendency to magnify minor and personally

unrelated tensions into proofs of purposeful deception and malice."[4]

David Shapiro observes: "A suspicious person is a person who has something on his mind. He looks at the world with fixed and preoccupying expectation, and he searches repetitively, and only, for confirmation of it. The fact is, furthermore, that their dismissal and disregard of anything that does not confirm their prior supposition is an active and intentional process."[5]

Suspicious people anticipate trickery. "What's he got up his sleeve?" Zophar railed, "Can you fathom the mysteries of God? Can you probe the limits of the Almighty?. . . What can you know?" (Job 11:7-8). Does that sound a lot like: "You think you know our community? You have been here two years. I have been in this church all my life. You do not know this church as I do. You will be gone in a couple of years. You will go on to a larger church. I will be here when you are gone. I am suspicious of your motives. I doubt your sincerity." We will call that person Zophar.

Not only do suspicious people anticipate trickery, but they also take excessive precautions. These persons are notorious for tabling a motion they do not agree with.

If mistakes are made during an event, they take a kind of "don't look at me!" attitude. They defer blame. They deny blame.

They have tunnel vision. Eliphaz asked Job: "What do you know that we do not know? What insights do you have that we do not have? The gray-haired and the aged are on our side, men even older than your father" (Job 15:9-10). In other words: "Don't bring your hair-brained ideas to us. We have already considered the future. No one could have a glimpse of the future that we have not calculated. We see what we want to see. We see the way things have already been done, and that's okay with us and for us."

Have you ever seen a suspicious person who could relax? Of course not. There are too many flaws to be found. There are too many glitches to be discovered. How can anyone relax when there is so much to be done. They even proof text their suspiciousness. Don't you know that the fields are white unto harvest already? Of course, it is taken out of context, but reason is not their forte.

These persons carry their feelings on their sleeves. They seem to look for reasons to be offended. Remember this: "Never fight with a pig. You both get dirty, and the pig likes it." When suspicious persons are offended, we are playing their game. They like it. They are good at it.

Practical Ways to Deal with Suspicious People

Job lost his historic and mythical patience in Job 12. (Of course, he never really had patience, just persistence.) He said, "Doubtless you are the people, and wisdom will die with you!" (v. 1). He became indignant: "But I have a mind as well as you; I am not inferior to you" (v. 2).

Avoid being intimidated.—Job was defensive, but he protected himself well. He suggested, "To God belong wisdom and power; counsel and understanding are his" (12:13). Bildad, Zophar, Eliphaz, and Elihu, just remember you do not own wisdom and power, counsel and understanding; but God does.

Avoid counterattack.—That is God's prerogative, not ours. Job came awfully close to this strategy. But strength in the face of adversity is our long suit. We must maintain dignity if we are to withstand the onslaught of suspicious persons.

Keep accurate records.—Suspicious persons distort the facts. A date book with recorded conversations can save a lot of grief when they eventually get into an "I said—you said" conversation.

Pray for them, and let them know you are praying for them.—Sanctimony will not work. Sanctimony is the attitude of "I know I am right, and I am praying for you because you are wrong and so suspicious." *Praying for them* means: "I am praying that I will not be so clumsy in our relationship. I know it is easy to for me to be misunderstood. Will you help me by praying for me, as well?" This relieves them of the pressure of the possibility of being wrong. It places more responsibility on us to be caring. No one said it was going to be easy.

The Circumferential Person

I borrowed the term from the prince of pastoral care, Dr. Wayne Oates, in his classic work, *The Care of Troublesome People.*[6] The circumferential person is also called "the backbiting person."

The Bible mentions this kind of person several times. In 1 Kings 19, Ahab is described as a tattletale. He wanted Jezebel to do the dirty work. So instead of taking action, which he had the authority to do, he told Jezebel about Elijah's exploits with the prophets of Baal. She was mean. She delighted in following up on the tattletale.

Paul probably considered Peter this kind of person (see Gal. 2:11-12). He said he stood "self-condemned" (NRSV)[7] because of his fear of the circumcision faction. Peter would later defend himself. Both men dealt with each other face-to-face.

The psychoanalyst, Karen Horney, described the basic sources of personal unhappiness as the "fundamentally contradictory attitudes [they have] acquired toward other persons."[8] These are movements. Moving toward people is the socially inclined person. Moving away from people is the isolationist. Moving against people is the head-on, negative person (Jezebel liked the conflict.); but circumferential persons move around people. They do it maliciously and intentionally. They strike behind people's backs.

Jesus spoke harshly about persons who slander others. "What comes out of a man is what makes him 'unclean.' For from within, out of men's hearts, come evil thoughts, sexual immorality, theft, murder, adultery, greed, malice, deceit, lewdness, envy, slander [*diabolos*, meaning "devilish" or "adversarial"], arrogance and folly. All these evils come from inside and make a man 'unclean'" (Mark 7:20-23).

Paul Meier wrote an amusing but provocative book, *Don't Let Jerks Get the Best of You: Advice for Dealing with Difficult People*. He called the circumferential person a "second-degree jerk" as opposed to a "first-degree jerk." He said that such a person will "spread gossip freely but tries to make it look as if she's 'really concerned' about the party being discussed."[9] He also said that the "jerk" "breaks traffic laws when he won't be caught, but doesn't intend to do any harm. . . . [He's] relatively honest, but tells lies with little, if any, guilt whenever it is more convenient to do so."[10]

A minister will recognize this statement: "I don't think we should try to reach that part of our community. I know this church better than most." (Of course, he means "better than you.") This person has the best interests of the church at heart.

Herschel Hobbs once said, "I never trust a layman who talks more spiritual than I do." He suspected an ulterior motive. My own prejudice on this matter is that there are a lot of frustrated pastors out there who pose as church lay leaders or deacons. They know much better than the pastor how to "run" a church. They "run" the church as subterranean pastors using the language of Zion more eloquently than the pastor and staff. It is convincing, but it is also demeaning to the pastor and staff. Backbiting is an art evidenced best when self-righteousness is the format.

In teaching young Timothy to be careful of these persons, Paul wrote, "If anyone teaches false doctrines and does not agree to the sound instruction of our Lord Jesus Christ and to godly teaching, he is conceited and understands nothing. He has an unhealthy interest in controversies and quarrels about words that result in envy, strife, malicious talk, evil suspicions and constant friction between men of corrupt mind, who have been robbed of the truth" (1 Tim. 6:3-5). Although the context is the love of money, the personality behavior is also applicable to the circumferential person. A backbiting person leaves the question in the mind of the caring pastor: "What do they really want?" This is not paranoia. They may really be out to get you. Fortunately, their numbers are not legion. Most persons recognize the deceitfulness of the circumferential person.

These persons are masterful in the use of calculated rumor. One of the best resources on the psychology of rumor was written by a Harvard professor more than 50 years ago. Gordon Allport wrote that rumor is a technique used in politics and society to gain the upper hand.[11] Rumor is best when it is vague, ambiguous, and confusing. In churches, I am always cautious when I hear the words, "I don't know this to be true, but I heard. . ." Such a statement creates just enough curiosity to make the listener want to believe it is true, and it becomes even more so when repeated.

Still another technique mastered by these persons is the misuse of legalities and/or parliamentary procedure. When this method is used, almost always someone has to lose. Jesus had several conversations with persons of the law. Entrapment was not foreign to the first century. An ideal church might be one that never had to take a vote but could reach every decision by consensus. No one loses. Everyone wins.

Practical Ways to Deal with Circumferential People

Paul came right to the point. "Flee from all this, and pursue righteousness, godliness, faith, love, endurance and gentleness" (1 Tim. 6:11). These matters have a way of disarming the circumferential person. This approach has a way of convincing circumferential persons that you will not be their ally.

A staff person had, on several occasions, brought disturbing information about another staff person to the pastor. "Would you like to hear the latest?" he began.

"Certainly," said the pastor, "but first, let's bring Jim in and let him have an opportunity to defend himself." He picked up the phone and asked Jim to step into his office. The rumor was about Jim and an administrative assistant. The pastor said he glanced at the person bringing the "latest" during the telephone call, and the blood had drained from his face. The issue was sensitive. It was not immoral, as the first staff person had assumed. One way to deal with the circumferential person is direct confrontation. It is not always advisable, but in this instance, appropriate.

One of the most memorable events, and in some ways most painful, that took place in a church where I was interim pastor was a result of third- or fourth-hand information. The young man acting as spokesman was the new chairman of deacons, acting, he felt, in the best interests of the church. I had been in the church as interim pastor once before for a period of two years after a forced termination of their pastor. This was the second time I had followed a forced termination of their pastor.

He asked for an appointment. I noticed his reluctance to look directly at me. "I am here on behalf of the deacons. Some have said we don't want you to talk about the termination of our pastor."

"Did they not want to talk to me?"

"They felt I should do the talking." Then, "We would like you to stop mentioning that our former pastor was terminated."

I think I would have wanted that too. One forced termination is often justified. Twice, and someone has to ask: Is this a pattern? Are circumstances in this church too uncomfortable to air?

"Would you mind asking this person to talk with me?"

"She would rather I talk for her," he said.

To this day, I have wondered how a "she" got into the conversation. The one thing I did learn is that some people would rather have others do the talking for them, especially if it is too painful for them to confront. Additionally, I learned that little can be done for the person who is willing to be used by backbiting persons.

Paul told Timothy, "Turn away from godless chatter and the opposing ideas of what is falsely called knowledge" (1 Tim. 6:20). That may be the best advice we can get about the circumferential person.

The Histrionic Person

The histrionic person is a visual showoff, "gratifying the cravings of our sinful nature and following its desires and thoughts" (Eph. 2:3). That would be a sorry plight if that were the end of the story. We are all histrionic to some degree. But that is not the end of the story. "But because of his great love for us, God, who is rich in mercy, made us alive with Christ even when we were dead in transgressions—it is by grace you have been saved" (Eph. 2:4-5).

There is hope. Difficult persons are not impossible. Grace means God is not finished. We are unfinished products because God is still at work in our lives.

Peter was a showoff, but he was also a rock. God can use even the most unsuspecting persons for His kingdom.

The histrionic person has an exaggerated expression of emotions. A sunset may be beautiful, but to the histrionic person it is a radiant expression of God's creative processes. They are poetic. They make the world interesting.

Aaron Beck has suggested they have feelings as follows: "Unless I captivate people, I am nothing." "If I can't entertain people, they will abandon me." "If people don't respond, they are rotten." "If I can't captivate people, I am helpless."[12]

On a more positive side: "He has a keen nose for anything new. Because he is always seeking out new possibilities, stable conditions suffocate him. He seizes on new objects or situations with great intensity. . . only to abandon them cold-bloodedly, without any compunction. . . as soon as their range is known."[13]

In a more lighthearted vein, someone suggested a topic on histrionic personalities could be "Getting Your Way by Screaming" or "Ego Gratification Through One-upmanship" or "Creative Anxiety."[14]

Paul probably showed a little histrionics when he said, "Let no one cause me trouble, for I bear on my body the marks of Jesus" (Gal. 6:17). While we applaud Paul for this farewell to the church at Galatia, we would probably caution a pastor or church staff person who would use that language. Today we might say, "Get off my back. I'm a minister." *Not* advisable.

One of the tiring aspects of histrionic persons is the incessant drawing of attention to themselves. A deacon joined me in visiting a cancer patient in the hospital. I had not spent enough time briefing him. (Never assume a person knows how to visit a hospital room with compassion, I later learned.)

While we were there, twice he tried to tell the cancer patient about his sister who had just gone through a similar operation and resulting treatments. Although he did not share the information, his sister passed away. His verbal skills were exceptional in the right context. But in this context they were out of control.

Histrionic persons appear warm and charming. Many are attractive people. But they can easily slip into a self-indulgent and inconsiderate mode of operation.

A performance appraisal is full of anxiety. It involves feedback, financial remuneration (or not), heart-to-heart talks with your manager, and planning for personal goal setting based on strategic priorities. There is no little preparation. A prominent trustee of the organization was visiting. It was a spontaneous visit, not a planned resource development visit. A mid-level manager was preparing for a performance appraisal of a lower-level manager. One of the up-line managers was being a good host. Needing support for the spontaneous visit, the up-line manager summoned the mid-level manager to help him host the trustee.

Upon learning the level of the person receiving the performance appraisal, the up-line manager disregarded the significance of the performance appraisal and called the mid-level manager away from the meeting for the rest of the day. "My needs are more important than the needs of underlings" was the message heard by the frustrated lower-level manager.

In a church, if a deacon gets more attention at the expense of interrupting a needy child who has asked for your time, it is inexcusable. Jesus gave His time to those who could not reward Him. No perks, no Holy Land tours, no possible financial remunerations could tempt Him away from tending to the sick, the lame, the blind, and the needy.

The histrionic person is demanding. This person craves activity and excitement. "Our church needs a new burst of energy; it is not growing. What can we do to help our church grow? Do we have the right leader for our church? Are we going in the right direction? Should we bring in a younger man to lead us?" Many terminations have been planted in their infancy by histrionic people who craved more for their church. Their vision is blurred by seeing activity as progress, by seeing excitement as production, and by seeing emotion as compassion.

Practical Ways of Dealing with Histrionic People

An efficient way to deal with histrionic persons is a theological issue. We must respect their human freedom. E. Y. Mullins wrote in 1917: "God's providential control of the world respects human freedom. . . . But man is on a higher level. God has limited himself in his methods with free beings."[15] Mullins made this statement in a discussion of the providence of God. God's providence is unstoppable. God's providence is not our responsibility. What does that mean in dealing with the histrionic person?

We cannot change the histrionic person. Start with that fact.

We can't change others. God's grace is always operative, but we cannot legislate it. God allows every person the opportunity for freedom. Everyone has the precious gift of free will. We cannot change that. We would not want to change it if we could. We cannot change those persons who interrupt the flow of the way we think things ought to be done. David recognized this: "Everything comes from you, and we have given you only what comes from your hand" (1 Chron. 29:14). The histrionic person frustrates, controls, distracts, and sometimes destroys. But God is in control. We cannot change these persons. Only God can do that. Why is this such a significant theological issue?

It is simple but profound. The histrionic person is stress inducing to the pastor and staff. You can hold them accountable. You can insist that they take responsibility. You can even encourage revocation in their work and personal relations. But you cannot change them. That is the magnificent feature of free will. Only God's grace can perform that miracle. Once we recognize that fact and learn to live with it, these persons are not nearly so difficult. Their destiny is not in our jurisdiction. Thank goodness.

Don't give in too quickly. Histrionic persons are demanding. Often this is accompanied by irrational, angry outbursts. To avoid the stress of conflict, we may give in too quickly. They already know this is a strong possibility. They have used this technique before, and it is has worked.

Practice controls. "Better a patient man than a warrior, a man who controls his temper than one who takes a city" (Prov. 16:32). We call children's actions pouting or sulking. For adults, we soften this description. We call it withdrawal. The technique is the same. The histrionic person wants his or her way. They are unaware of the insistent nature of this pattern. When encountering histrionic people, patience is more than a virtue. It is a necessity.

Children are histrionic by nature. They incessantly draw attention to themselves. They crave activity and excitement. They constantly seek reassurance. But we expect more of the mature adult. We are often disappointed. Here we need controls. Here we need patience and the control of our temper.

The Star Performer

We have borrowed Dr. Oates term to describe this person. Millon called this person "narcissistic."[16]

The star performer wants to be the bride at every wedding,

the corpse at every funeral. Okay, that is a worn-out cliche, but the meaning is apparent. They want to be front and center.

Too often, they ignore others' needs. A sense of entitlement is prevalent. Marked feelings of expectation escalate when entitlement is missing. This person is the albatross of the minister of music. If the star performer is in the choir, he or she expects to sing a solo frequently.

Rules are necessary. They just don't apply to *them*. Their situation is different. They are not like others. They have "special" needs, wants, and desires. This entitles them to a special set of circumstances. Professional athletes are notorious for getting away with things that others would be imprisoned for. Politicians do not see their guilt in perjury in the same light as ordinary citizens.

They know things and people others do not know. This affords them special privileges. They have had things revealed to them that others could not possibly know. They see no contradiction in their Christianity that others do not have access to the same light. John was cryptic in his assessment of these kinds of difficult persons: "Anyone who claims to be in the light but hates his brother is still in the darkness. Whoever loves his brother lives in the light, and there is nothing in him to make him stumble. But whoever hates his brother is in the darkness and walks around in the darkness; he does not know where he is going, because the darkness has blinded him" (1 John 2:9-11).

Making it doubly difficult for the pastor, these persons are preoccupied with fantasies of unlimited success in their church. "Our church can be the biggest in this city. Our pastor can be the best. Our recreation program will be second to none." In itself, nothing is wrong with these feelings. But when these feelings become preeminent in the achievement standards for the pastor, they become difficult. The response becomes: "Why isn't our church the biggest in this city? What is wrong with our pastor that others are not attracted to his preaching? Why do people get involved in other churches when we have these extraordinary recreation facilities?"

Otto Kernberg gave this scathing summation of star performers, or narcissistic persons: "They envy others, tend to idealize some people from whom they expect narcissistic supplies, and to depreciate and treat with contempt those from whom they do not expect anything (often their former idols). In general, their relationships with other people are clearly exploitative and sometimes parasitic. It is as if they feel they have the right to control and possess others and to exploit them without guilt feelings—and behind a surface which very often is charming and engaging, one senses coldness and ruthlessness."[17]

Paul had much experience with these persons. He warned Titus, "Avoid foolish controversies and genealogies and arguments and quarrels about the law, because these are unprofitable and useless. Warn a divisive peron once, and then warn him a second time. After that, have nothing to do with him. You may be sure that such a man is warped and sinful; he is self-condemned" (Titus 3:9-11).

Practical Ways to Deal with Star Performers

Be fair.—Treat them as you would others, without preferential treatment. But also treat them as well as you do others. The tendency is to pull away from them. That would not be fair either.

Remember the theological premise of personal freedom.—You cannot change them; only God can do that.

Love them.—They are hard to love. Paul's advice to "have nothing to do with them" means to avoid becoming a subject of their exploitation. Do not let them possess or control you. Learn to say no. You can say no with warmth but still be firm. We are still encouraged to love them.

Look for the escape valves.—Close friends and allies in the church can help you deal with star performers by occupying them in other areas. Communicate with these friends about your need to have them distracted into meaningful activities which will free you from their constant demands of your attention.

Pray for patience.—And be patient while you pray for patience. It may be a long time coming.

The Passive-Aggressive Person

I always think of Judas as being passive-aggressive. He was secretive and devious. He wanted something different from Jesus than the purpose of God. He had the power of the purse, and too often persons responsible for the purse become possessive. "This is my money" is not an uncommon feeling. Perhaps Judas assumed more responsibility than he was entitled to and became provoked that things did not move in the direction he wished.

Jonah was passive-aggressive. When he was placed in an embarrassing position, rather than face the music, he whined, "O LORD, take away my life, for it is better for me to die than to live" (Jon. 4:3).

I have been passive-aggressive on more occasions than I wish to admit. Some of the characteristics I have displayed are:

- Procrastination—I put off things I did not want to do.
- Inefficiency—"I did not think of this, so it must be second class."
- Forgetfulness—"It is not worth remembering because it is not mine."
- Hidden agendas—"I wish he would quit talking; then I could discuss something really interesting."

Passive-aggressive people carefully hide their true feelings. One of my favorite couple stories goes like this:

"I was a fool when I married you," he complained.

She said, "Yes, but I didn't know it then."

They are secretive to a fault. Every game is played close to the vest. And life to them is a game.

Another great story was a letter written to a preacher: "Dear Preacher, You are a mealy mouthed, chicken-livered coward. You never take a stand on anything. You're afraid to be held accountable for your opinion or your actions. You lack the guts to state the truth. Well, I say, 'Put up or shut up.' Yours truly, Anonymous." That gives an accurate description of the passive-aggressive.

Passive-aggressive behavior is distinguishable from depression, although some of the characteristics are similar. They do, however, have many things in common. "The depressives see themselves as failures because they do not, or did not, live up to expectations of themselves or those placed there by others."[18] Passive-aggressives, on the other hand, see others as failures because others do not, or did not, live up to expectations which have been superimposed on them by the passive-aggressive.

Depression is primarily turned-in anger. Passive-aggressive behavior is anger internalized but felt to be caused by others. Depression is notably distinguishable by guilt. The good news is that with treatment depression has access to God's grace. With passive aggression, the wall of denial is often so high these persons shut out access to God's grace. Our job often becomes one of trying to break through these barriers.

Depressive people are also difficult, but they fit into an altogether different category. Depression is an illness. It is often physiologically traceable. Therefore, it is treatable. It is distinguishable by many levels of diagnosis. Clinically, it moves from manic depression, to major depression, to acute depression, to episodic, or periodic depression. Almost all levels of clinical depression are treatable. Pastors should have the appropriate expertise to know when they are in over their heads in dealing with depression and should know when, how, and where to refer depressed persons to therapists.

Passive-aggressive behavior is seductive. Ministers are helpers by nature. We want to help those who are skilled at putting distance between us. We also want to erase the distance. Many of us consider that a magnificent accomplishment. Some ministers become emotionally, even physically involved with passive-aggressive persons because we want to save them. (Of course, only God can do that.) They throw out the bait with an "I dare you" attitude to see if you can get through their emotional shield. We accept it as a challenge. In legalese, it is called *entrapment*. We are entrapped by their seductive skill of passive aggression. We search for the morsels of accolades from them because they are so hard to find. It is similar to hunting an elusive animal. There is great victory in searching out their hiding place of emotional deprivation. Before we come up for air into the reality of living, we are sometimes captured in the sordid web of an adulterous relationship with one of the most dangerous behavior patterns possible. Many ministers have been embarrassed and legally charged with improper behavior because they would not see the dangers of passive aggression from church members or persons with whom they minister.

Passive-aggressive behavior is behavior pastors and staff must deal with on a daily basis. Some of the behavior patterns are carryovers from childhood, and church members who adopt passive-aggressive behavior are unaware of their own patterns. This makes it even more difficult to deal with them, because their denial reverses the blame to the other person. Rarely will you hear the words "I was wrong" or "You were right" come from the person who is passive-aggressive. Depressive persons use these words with candor and frequency. But, unfortunately, this feeling of being wrong does nothing to deter the irresponsible and/or inappropriate behavior.

Practical Ways to Deal with Passive-Aggressive People
First, recognize them as powerful and seductive people. Look for the danger signals. Remember God's grace, but act with caution. Then act responsibly. God expects us to act with the good com-

mon sense He has enabled us to have.

Millon and others call the passive-aggressive the "avoidant" personality. He "expects to be degraded and humiliated by people, and so he or she refuses any assignments that might involve increased interpersonal contact."[19] Therefore, the pastor and staff person working with this person must be careful in callous chatting or "kidding around" with them. They are overly sensitive.

They have a tendency to feel "I'm different," or "I don't fit in," or "I must be different —that's why I have no friends."[20]

If Judas had been passive-aggressive, it would give profound meaning to Jesus' statement, "What you are about to do, do quickly" (John 13:27). The passive-aggressive procrastinate. They put things off. They drag their feet. Whether this tendency is to get attention or to block the progress of the leader, it is, in any case, frustrating. Jesus was saying: "Get it over with. Do your treacherous deed. Do it quickly."

To the degree that they are teachable, passive-aggressive persons need to experience God's grace. Jesus said, "Peace I leave with you; my peace I give you. I do not give to you as the world gives. Do not let your hearts be troubled and do not be afraid" (John 14:27). They need God's grace and God's peace. The self-assurance given by God's grace can solve many troubling moods.

In every passive-aggressive pattern, a storm seems to be brewing. It finds expression in anger, rage, stubbornness, inefficiency, and ineffectiveness. The peace given by God's Holy Spirit can be modeled by the pastor and staff. Perhaps the deeds they must perform can be tempered by the grace of God and the peace given by His Holy Spirit.

The Borderline Personality

"When Reuben heard this, he tried to rescue him from their hands. 'Let's not take his life,' he said. 'Don't shed any blood. Throw him into this cistern here in the desert, but don't lay a hand on him.' Reuben said this to rescue him from them and take him back to his father" (Gen. 37:21-22). Reuben was not a hero. He abdicated the leadership role and wimped out. He may have decided, too late, to avoid the bloodshed; but he still was attempting to make his father responsible for Joseph's safety. Of course, it did not work. Reuben may have been the classic borderline personality of the Old Testament. He had some honor left. But remember, he had been in on the group decision from the beginning.

Borderline personality is distinguishable by ambivalent and erratic behavior. These persons keep making the same decisions over and over again. They decide for it. Then they decide against it.

They are unstable in interpersonal behavior, mood, and self-image. Willie Loman, in Tennessee William's *Death of a Salesman*, ultimately died a tragic death. A son stood over his corpse and half-eulogized: "Poor Dad. He never really knew who he was." Borderline persons show unpredictable behavior in spending, sex, gambling, substance abuse, shoplifting, and/or overeating. Why? Because they are always on the borderline of doing the right thing, but it just comes out wrong. They do not know who they are.

Pilate was on the verge of doing the right thing with Jesus, but he succumbed. He listened to the crowd and lamented, "I am innocent of this man's blood. . . . It is your responsibility!" (Matt. 27:24). He was on the borderline.

How many good persons have listened to the crowd? "He is not preaching to our needs." "He cannot get along with the key people in the church." "He is lazy." "He is not like our former pastor." "I am the biggest giver in this church, and he rarely ever speaks to me."

The borderline person listens and says: "Let's not kill him. Let's give him three months' salary and turn him out to pasture. After all, he is 57 years old, and in just a few years more he can collect Social Security." It isn't right.

Emil Kraepelin wrote that borderline persons "display from youth up extraordinarily great fluctuations in emotional equilibrium and are greatly moved by all experiences, frequently in an unpleasant way. . . . They flare up, and on the most trivial occasions fall into outbursts of boundless fury. . . . The coloring of mood is subject to frequent change. . . . They are mostly very distractible and unsteady in their endeavors."[21]

They have a compulsive need for reassurance. It is especially evident in reoccurring guilt from falling short in religious events or religious experiences. Some have called the persons who have a need for rededication in public, week after week, "repeat offenders." These persons never really get enough reassurance from knowing that God has forgiven them of their sin and that they are living in the grace which was placed in their religious experience. They have cheap grace because they do not experience its permanence. Their fault, certainly not God's.

Practical Ways to Deal with Borderline People

Unexpected gestures of reassurance confirm their worth. "I was thinking about how important you are to the work of our church."

Try to avoid being intimidated when outbursts of inappropriate behavior occur. If it is anger, a soft answer turns away wrath. If it is bizarre behavior, try not to be too surprised. Anticipate the unexpected.

Affirm their rededication. But do more than pray for them in the public gathering. Meet with them individually during the week, away from the worship experience, and affirm the fact that God forgives and you believe that He forgives them.

Build a support group for this person. Many of these persons can help one another. Of course, the chemistry has to be right, and that is why you are getting paid the big bucks: to make these kinds of evaluations. Pray that God will help you decide on a good course of action for them. Many of them want to be used of God but are not willing to take the risk of asking for a specific responsibility.

Guidelines for Working with Difficult People

Be assertive, but not aggressive.—Edward Crutchfield, the CEO of First Union Corporation, tried to win over employees after his firm acquired a series of regional banks. He opened his remarks with, "I bet no one here has the guts to ask me an insulting question." If your tendency is to be blustery, work on charm. People are fun to be with if you let them.

Clarify, but avoid contradicting.—"You are wrong" and "That's not right" are statements that are bound to alienate. Try: "Let me see if I understand what you are saying." "Say a word more on that." "I believe some could see it that way." "Do you think there are other options?"

Develop controls.—Recognize your own clay feet. Know your theological Achilles' heel. Know when you are in over your head. Defer when necessary. You don't have to have all the answers.

Develop the power to wait before you react to a volatile situation.—The courage to speak is not nearly as important as the patience not to speak.

Work on your technical skills.—Learn more about difficult behavior patterns and how to understand them. Then you will be more patient in working with them.

If things aren't right at home, don't get involved in messy situations in the church.—Start at home. Get things right with your spouse, children, extended family; then you will be more suited to solving problems with difficult persons in the church.

Avoid the trap of "I am the only one who can help this person."—You may not be able to help this person. It could be that there is a person more capable of helping than you. Know your limitations. Understand your possibilities.

Remember that the primary problem is almost always secondary.—What the difficult person is having problems with is almost always in the second paragraph. Be patient and wait for the full story, and you will be a knight in shining armor for those who think no one understands them.

Ask yourself, "W.W.J.D.?"—The kids know it. Adults should. It is still a great practice. Work on the premise, "What would Jesus do?"

---

[1] Scott Peck, *People of the Lie* (New York: Simon & Schuster, 1983), 72.

[2] *Holman Bible Dictionary*, ed. Trent Butler (Nashville: Holman, 1991), 197.

[3] Binford W. Gilbert, *The Pastoral Care of Depression: A Guidebook* (New York: Haworth Pastoral Press, 1998), 103.

[4] Theodore Millon with Roger D. Davis, *Disorders of Personality DSM-IV and Beyond* (New York: John Wiley and Sons, 1996), 698.

[5] David Shapiro, *Neurotic Styles* (New York: Basic Books, 1965), 57, as quoted in Millon and Davis, 695.

[6] Wayne Oates, *The Care of Troublesome People* (Bethesda, MD: Alban Institute, 1994), 15ff.

[7] From the *New Revised Standard Version of the Bible,* copyright © 1989 by the Division of Christian Education of the National Council of Churches of Christ in the United States of America. Used by permission. All rights reserved.

[8] Oates, 15.

[9] Paul Meier, *Don't Let Jerks Get the Best of You: Advice for Dealing with Difficult People* (Nashville: Thomas Nelson, 1994), 45.

[10] Ibid., 46.

[11] Gordon Allport, *The Psychology of Rumor* (New York: Henry Holt Publishers, 1947).

[12] A. T Beck and A. Freeman, *Cognitive Therapy of Personality Disorders* (New York: Guilford, 1990), 50, as quoted in Millon and Davis, 362.

[13] C. G. Jung, *Psychological Types* (Zurich: Rasher Verlag, 1921), 368, as quoted in Millon and Davis, 359.

[14] See Nancy Loving Tubesing and Sandy Steward Christian, *Structured Exercises in Wellness Promotion,* vol. 5 (Duluth, MN: Whole Person Press), 123.

[15] E. Y. Mullins, *The Christian Religion in Its Doctrinal Expression* (Philadelphia: Judson Press, 1917), 268.

[16] Millon and Davis, 394.

[17] Otto F. Kernberg, "Borderline Personality Organization," *Journal of the American Psychoanalytic Association,* 15 (1967): 655, as quoted in Millon and Davis, 397.

[18] Binford Gilbert, *The Pastoral Care of Depression: A Guidebook* (New York: Haworth Press, 1998), 24.

[19] Lorna Benjamin, *Interpersonal and Treatment of Personality Disorders* (New York: Guilford, 1993), 300, as quoted in Millon and Davis, 257.

[20] Beck and Freeman, 261, as quoted in Millon and Davis, 257.

[21] Emil Kraepelin, *Manic-Depressive Insanity and Paranoia* (Edinborough: Livingstone, 1921), 130, as quoted in Millon and Davis, 648.

AVOIDING THE BLOWHARD SYNDROME

TIPS

1	Learning to listen is harder than learning to speak.
2	Wisdom is timing—when to speak, when to listen.
3	If you speak more than four minutes without listening in a dialogue, it isn't.
4	"He who loves a quarrel loves sin" (Prov. 17:19).
5	Repeat what you have learned, not what you have said.
6	Stopping is more difficult for the preacher than starting. If you say, "My final point is. . . ," then mean it.
7	Most sermons delivered in 50 minutes are more convincing in 30.
8	The invitation given in a worship service is a significant time of shared communication between God and people. It should be handled as an awesome period of the presence of God.
9	Mannerisms which distract from the message are unnecessary.
10	Speak distinctly.
11	You don't have to defend the Bible. It defends itself.
12	Respect your listeners. They deserve it.

"Dear brothers, don't ever forget that it is best to listen much, speak little, and not become angry" (Jas. 1:19, TLB).

"I have one piece of advice," he said, "I'm glad you have been called to ministry, but just don't be a blowhard." He was the cynical deacon who angered my Dad with his comment when George Bugg, my pastor, told Varner River Baptist Church I had been called to ministry. John was skeptical of my call.

The day John gave me the advice was a celebration. I was affirmed. How many times does a church running 75 in Sunday School have a 16-year-old called to ministry? I thought John's advice was good. Dad didn't like it. Dad heard a criticism of his son.

A few years later when I was in seminary, and my wife and I were struggling financially, I received a check, a sizable amount from John. "Don't pay this back," the note said. "I am proud of you. Keep up the good work. John."

Some people talk because they have something to say. Some talk until they think of something to say. Some people hear because they want to know what is being said. Some listen as an interval to allow them to think of what to say. People in this last group prompted John's remark about blowhards. I don't want to be a self-serving preacher full of hot air. You don't either.

Why are some people boring and others interesting? Why can two people say virtually the same thing, and and one is heard and the other is dismissed before ever speaking? Communicating is the minister's most complex skill and perhaps the most essential in sharing the good news of Christ. *Lord, help me to be heard, but help me say something worth hearing.*

Listen First

Verbal skills are vital. They help make a preacher effective. They help the minister of education enlist volunteers. They give the minister of music a way to enlist choir members. But verbal skills are not the most essential ingredient in communication.

When Jesus was before the Sanhedrin, the inflammatory questions were coming at rapid-fire speed. "Are you not going to answer? What is this testimony that these men are bringing against you?" (Matt. 26:62).

Did Jesus prepare a brief to defend Himself? Did He build a 400-page document to prove His innocence? Did He hire a parade of lawyers to establish His messianic reign? No. "But Jesus remained silent" (Matt. 26:63).

The high priest said, "Tell us if you are the Christ, the Son of God." Then Jesus said, "Yes, it is as you say" (Matt. 26:63-64).

Listening permits others to position themselves. Every person learns at his or her own pace. Few learn by persuasion. Motivational experts are entertaining, but only rarely are life-changing decisions made as a result of motivational persuasion. All of us must have teachable moments. Most of mine have come as a result of someone listening to me. Listening communicates compassion, concern, and care. Persuasion gives the impression that we are not what we ought to be, that we do not have what we ought to have. Of course, those who are lost need persuading that they are lost. Listening is supportive and affirming.

People can be won to Christ when the Holy Spirit prepares them. The Holy Spirit works through human events. He convicts of sin. Our skill as communicators must excel at knowing how and when the Holy Spirit is at work. To do that we must stay in touch with the Holy Spirit. I always feel uncomfortable when persons take credit for "winning people to Christ." I have felt Proverbs 11:30, "He who wins souls is wise," should be a private victory not a public proclamation. I prefer the expression, "leading persons to a saving knowledge of Jesus Christ." The one who finds Christ is the one who wins. I would rather be an instrument that helps others find the Lord, to help them hear their own words: "I think I need the Lord." Then it is time for Romans 3:23, Romans 6:23, John 3:16, Romans 8:6, and John 20:29. Modeling the compassion and love of Christ is superior to excellent articulation skills. To articulate the message of Christ is necessary. Living the spirit of Christ is indispensable.

"He who answers before listening—that is his folly and his

shame" (Prov. 18:13). "Listen to advice and accept instruction, and in the end you will be wise" (Prov. 19:20).

The psalmist prayed, "Give ear to my words, O LORD, consider my sighing. Listen to my cry for help" (Ps. 5:1-2). People want to be around someone who will listen. People want to be heard. The best way to tell people about Christ is to hear their hurt and point them to the One who can relieve their pain. Christ forgives sin. That is what persons want and need—God's grace.

Several messages are possible: (1) what the person intends to say, (2) what the person actually says, (3) what the person is understood to say, (4) what the hearer wants to hear, (5) what the hearer actually hears, and (6) what communication and understanding actually take place after the discourse and exchange. Someone has dramatized communication problems this way: I know you believe you understand what you think I said, but I am not sure you realize that what you heard is not what I meant.

Communicating the Message of Christ

In 1974, in the original version of *Getting on Top of Your Work*, we designed the patterns of communication as follows:

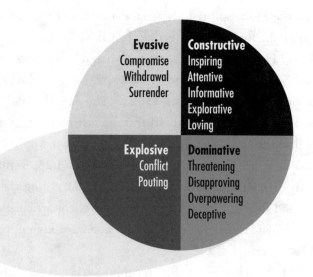

Since that time, communication patterns have evolved to other dimensions. In the old model, the characteristics were overly judgmental. It appeared the only "right" pattern was constructive. However, different situations call for different patterns. The 8th-century prophets were not always constructive, but they were effective. We have had to take a long, hard look at the communication patterns which might best equip ministers for the 21st century. Not all work the same way. Not all work in the same places. But each of the patterns is preferable in certain situations.

The 21st-century descriptions are:

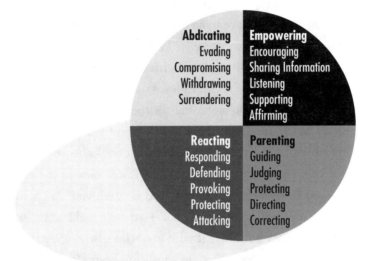

Empowering

E. Y. Mullins said: "The best service which Christianity can render to society is to produce righteousness in individual character and at the same time set the man free as an agent of righteousness in society at large."[1] The autonomy of the church, a historical tenet in Baptist life, is foundational for the priesthood of every believer. These two factors, autonomy of the church and the priesthood of every believer, are the empowering forces of God's kingdom enterprise.

Empowering could be as simple as one who releases the power to behave responsibly and redemptively as opposed to those who restrict the power to behave individualistically.

Encouraging.—The communication pattern which empowers encourages others. Encouragers have a kind of built-in radar to know when and how to say the right things. They know how to "push the right buttons."

My Dad has been dead for 37 years. My brother, at 80, has the right to say just about anything he wants to say to me because he has become a kind of surrogate dad. Those few times where accolades were measurably conspicuous—in a Baptist Press release or the release of a book, I have looked forward to his response. It is a memorable moment when he says, "I am proud of you."

Encouraging is also helping to lighten the load. When Jethro, Moses' father-in-law "saw all that Moses was doing for the people, he said, 'What is this you are doing for the people? Why do you alone sit as judge, while all these people stand around you from morning till evening?'" (Ex. 18:14). He went on. "The work is too heavy for you; you cannot handle it alone. Listen now to me and I will give you some advice, and may God be with you. . . . Select capable men from all the people. . . . That will make your load lighter, because they will share it with you" (Ex. 18:18-19, 21-22).

"Listen to me, Moses. You are spreading yourself too thin. I want the father of my grandchildren to have a long and rewarding life. Lighten up. Give others room to operate. Give your job away. And don't nitpick after you have given it. Let others make their own mistakes. They probably won't do the job as well as you. But they will get it done because they are trustworthy." That's what he would have said if he had been living in the year 2000.

I have a feeling that Moses grieved over that advice from Jethro, but he knew Jethro was concerned about his welfare.

Rex Horne, pastor, Immanuel Baptist, Little Rock, wrote in his September 16, 1998 column in *The Record* an article entitled

"Encouragers." He wrote, "Karen Reed sent me some letters from children to their pastors that brightened my day:

"Dear Pastor, I know God loves everybody, but he never met my sister. Arnold. Age 8.

"Dear Pastor, Please say in your sermon that Peter Peterson has been a good boy all week. I am Peter Peterson. Age 9.

"Dear Pastor, I liked your sermon on Sunday. Especially when it was finished. Ralph. Age 11."[2]

Encouragement is being able to push the right button. Sometimes it is the humor button. Sometimes it is the lighten-up button. There are many more. What are some of yours?

Sharing Information.—Sharing information, especially sensitive information, is a matter of trust. It is a way of showing others they are valued. Sharing information is a way of encompassing all into the realm of solutions. But it is also makes us vulnerable. Vulnerable persons are more approachable. Eli thought Hannah was drunk because of her bizarre behavior. "'Not so, my lord,'" Hannah replied, 'I am a woman who is deeply troubled. I have not been drinking wine or beer; I was pouring out my soul to the LORD. Do not take your servant for a wicked woman. . . .' Eli answered, 'Go in peace, and may the God of Israel grant you what you have asked of him'" (1 Sam. 1:15-17). Hannah made herself vulnerable, and it was subject to being misunderstood, but Eli ended his suspicion by giving her a blessing.

Listening.—Our vocation as preacher is talking. Is it any wonder we have difficulty listening? We are gifted at talking. We have to learn to listen. It is not a natural or normal behavior. It takes concentration, patience, and preoccupation with others.

James said, "Everyone should be quick to listen, slow to speak and slow to become angry. . . . If anyone considers himself religious and yet does not keep a tight rein on his tongue, he deceives himself and his religion is worthless" (Jas. 1:19, 26).

Token support is a term used in management for those who wish to avoid losing their job but are not willing to support the goals superimposed on them by upper management. No one is lazy except in the pursuit of someone else's goals and objectives. When goals, objectives, and strategic priorities are superimposed, it usually means token support by those in the "grunt" areas. The ditches are dug at a rate determined by the workers, not the supervisors—or pastors, for that matter.

Events which get token support occur when listening is limited. A three-hour meeting which gives a platform for one or two persons to talk is not motivational. A minister of education who gives enrollment and attendance goals to the Sunday School director but allows no time for feedback must hope the warmth of the relationship carries some positive flow. Because the process will dampen the "want to" unless the director really "likes" the minister of education.

Go back to the first subtopic in this chapter. Listening is the indispensable ingredient for getting through to persons.

Supporting.—Much has been made of the word *civility* in this decade. Some have interpreted the idea of civility as approval or license. A minister must not give the impression of approving sin, but the idea of supporting an individual is a way of affirming a person's worth. It is possible to hate the sin but love the sinner. We can communicate support as a way of bringing that person into a restorative relationship to the love of Christ. Civility is being courteous, kind, considerate. It does not mean you agree. It simply means you are being decent, civil, and supportive.

Affirming.—One of the sweetest episodes of maternal support to Jesus was at the wedding at Cana. They ran out of wine. Mary said, "They have no more wine."

Jesus resisted. "My time has not yet come."

Mary said to the servants, "Do whatever he tells you."

She laid the foundation for Jesus, and later the Scriptures say, "He thus revealed his glory" (John 2:3, 4, 5, 11). Jesus turned the water into choice wine and performed His first miracle. Mary affirmed His deity by leaving the choice up to Him. She called the best in Him. She laid the foundation for His holiness and righteousness. It was a crowning moment in the Christian doctrinal expression of God being in Christ, reconciling the world unto Himself. The miracle event, His first, established Him as God's Son.

My grandson Zach sat listening to me complain about my own ineptness. I had misplaced my wife's prescription, and I had already bungled about three other chores. I had cut my hand on the dishwasher. I had dropped a lamp, and now I was having a "senior moment" by losing a prescription.

To no one in particular, I said, "I am not worth two cents!"

My six-year-old grandson heard me talking, and said, "Paw-paw, you're worth a million dollars to me." I was affirmed.

Other ways to affirm persons are:

"I was wrong!"

"You were right!"

"Thank you."

"You look great."

"I appreciate you."

"You have a gift for saying the right thing at the right time."

"I wish I had your patience."

Make your own list.

Parenting

Twenty five years ago, we gave this link in communication "dominative." That is unfair. *Dominative* has negative connotations. *Parenting* has positive connotations. *Parenting* means you care for a person enough to help him or her make choices. Sometimes in communicating the love of Christ, this is essential. Paul said, "To Titus, my true son in our common faith" (Titus 1:4). Earlier he wrote, "To Timothy my true son in the faith" (1 Tim. 1:2).

Throughout Paul's letters, he used parental language. "Live at peace with each other" (1 Thess. 5:13). He gives parental instructions to family members in Colossians 3:18-22.

Guiding.—Perhaps the simplest message of parental communication was interpreted by the MIT and Harvard Business School scholar Robert K. Greenleaf: "I also know that the well-being of the other person may depend on a constructive tension that I may be able to create; therefore, I must weigh my responsibility for saying the words or taking the actions that will bring this tension about."[3] That is parental tension which "guides." "Gentleness, in itself, is not always kindness. The act may seem hard and unreasonable to the recipient at the time, but it may be the most constructive kindness."[4]

As Greenleaf develops his thesis, we begin to see overlapping meaning for the minister in a guiding relationship with a church. The tension is in knowing when to push and when to pull. Guiding in parental communication is the genius of knowing when.

Judging.—Judging implies a value statement: "This is good." "This is bad." As prophets of God, we are responsible for interpreting sin. We must call sin, "sin." Sin is not a mistake, a glitch, an irresponsible act. No, sin is sin. The Bible is clear. There are times to be judicial about sin. We must, however, be careful that judging sin is not condemning the person. In the context of judging sin, Paul said, "In your anger do not sin" (Eph. 4:26). He added, "Be kind and compassionate to one another, forgiving each other, just as in Christ God forgave you" (Eph. 4:32).

In the sit-com *Seinfeld*, several scripts were built around the "soup nazi." This was a person who decided who should have his soup. He was loud, abrasive, and scary, to the *Seinfeld* cast. He was constantly making "judgments" about who was entitled.

I have often asked myself if I come across as a "pulpit nazi." Am I so loud that I turn off discriminating listeners?

I don't want children to leave a worship service, asking their parents, "Who was he mad at?" I don't want to be a blowhard.

On the other hand, I don't want people to go away thinking I was soft on sin. After a sermon interpreting Romans 1:27, and the verses following, a woman confronted me. "There are some things in the Bible that are better left alone," she said. "I thought we had come too far for preachers to talk about gay persons as if homosexuality was a sin." Her statement startled me. She carried a larger story than I knew. It was not simply about what I had called sin; it was much broader and deeper.

Protecting.—A parent protects his or her child. A communication pattern of protecting avoids gossip and stands in the gap between one person and those in the line of fire or attack. Protecting is more a feeling than a behavior. Some persons just make you feel safer when you are around them. It is an attitude.

Directing.—Sometimes ministers must be directive. It is not enough to straddle the fence when the game is on the line. You must call a play. It is uncomfortable. Chances of irritating at least some are high. But it is necessary.

In *The Charismatic Leader*, under "Empowering Others to Achieve the Dream," Jay Conger suggested that the first thing effective persons lose in the mentality of a bureaucracy is their sense of power. He talked it up. He renewed their sense of contribution. He directed them into thinking they had the power to change things. When we think of "directing," we usually think of correcting, but directing can be positive. He directed them to recognize that each person can make a difference. He established the "I Make a Difference Club" in each of the factories where he worked as leader. He directed their energies to accomplish more than they thought they could accomplish.[5]

In the parental image we paint in the pulpit, we would do well to learn from this McGill University professor. We can direct persons to assume the responsibility of leading others to a saving knowledge of Christ. We can direct people to love and forgive and understand and be compassionate.

Correcting.—"There is no one righteous, not even one" (Rom. 3:10). "So be careful with your self-righteous attitude and condemnation of others," I have said many times to myself. We have a right to correct the Pharisees; I just don't want to be one of them. There is a time to correct. "There is a way that seems right to a man, but in the end it leads to death" (Prov. 16:25).

Parenting can be used in communication as a way of controlling. Parenting may be an assumption that "I know what is best for others." This is an abuse of the communication system. But parenting can be used as a means of communication because you "want what is best for others," and in this case it is constructive.

Reacting

Some ministers are not actors so much as reactors. Jay Conger, in *The Charismatic Leader*, discussed a CEO who was questioned about his vision for his company. He suggested that he became involved in the day-to-day activities when he was still in middle management and, over a period of time, adopted the philosophy and strategic priorities of his company. The result was that when he became CEO he already had a philosophy of management. He knew what should be done in areas of product line and resource development. In other words, he reacted to his environment.[6]

Some react as a way of communicating. It is not necessarily a detriment to leadership. In fact, it may be redemptive. These persons communicate with the skill and knowledge of the awareness of their surroundings. "The wise in heart are called discerning, and pleasant words promote instruction" (Prov. 16:21).

Of course, there is a down side. Some reactors wait for others to position themselves in order to get the upper hand. This has devious implications and makes for unpleasant surroundings. Teamwork demands respect for every person who is contributing.

Responding.—One of the rules for whitewater rafting is "Go with the flow and don't get rattled." It works in Baptist churches as well. You can react without exploding. It is not easy. Nothing worth doing is easy. A response without a ballistic attack shows warmth. Responding is a way to show respect.

Recently, I ran across what one staff person thought was an oxymoron in a Baptist church—"a brief meeting." If he is correct, and I think he is, one reason is that the reactor is more defensive than responsive. Defending a position takes a great deal of time. It takes only a few moments to respond to a position stated clearly, even if we do not agree. Again, I like the word *civility*, even though it has been contaminated as "tolerance," because it responds warmly to the command to "be kind" (Eph. 4:32).

Defending.—Some things are worth defending. Right should be defended. Morality should be defended. Overbearing persons will run roughshod over leaders if they do not defend the positions of righteousness. People should not be terminated because they are not liked. Termination should be only for just cause. Pastors should defend their staff even if it jeopardizes their strength with some power persons in the church. Loyalty will not be won unless it is tested. The long-term results are indispensable.

Provoking.—The reactor in communication may, on occasion, be provocative. It may be for just cause. It may be simply because of some behavior problems of their own. Those who are provocative do not always know they are being provocative. It has become a pattern. We discussed this at length in chapter 3.

These brief stories are about two golfers. One provokes. One comforts. The image of one of my heroes was tainted when he responded provocatively to a fan. The fan yelled, "Way to go, _____! You're the man." In front of millions of persons, he turned and walked defiantly toward the fan. "Why don't you learn to be quiet? Then we would all be 'the man.'" It is not necessary to discuss the fact that he hit a bad shot. Commentator Johnny Miller was literally speechless and embarrassed for the golfer.

The second golfer is David Frost. In a recent tournament,

John Daly had walked off the green with chills. He has had problems with alcoholism. Frost, who was competing with him, walked to the next tee with his arm around him. The comforting gesture was carried in a photo in *Sports Illustrated.*[7] That is a different kind of provocation. I was provoked to tears by the latter. I was provoked to irritation by the first.

Protecting.—It could be said that David Frost was protecting John Daly from the unmerciful criticism of the press. This would have been true, too. Protecting is a way of reacting. The minister with a reacting mentality of compassion shows protection signals.

Attacking.—There is a time to attack. When a child is abused, the atrocity should be attacked verbally and legally. A positive side effect of the reactor communicator is that we have these persons to withstand the onslaught of evil. The downside is that sometimes the characteristic is misguided if overcompulsive.

The reacting pattern of communication is not easily channeled. Fortunately, many have learned to use this skill redemptively and effectively.

Abdicating

The youngest of Job's four friends was Elihu, the last to speak. He abdicated by deferring to those who should have been wiser as well as older. "I am young in years, and you are old; that is why I was fearful, not daring to tell you what I know. I thought, 'Age should speak; advanced years should teach wisdom.' But it is the spirit in a man, the breath of the Almighty, that gives him understanding. . . . While you were searching for words, I gave you my full attention" (Job 32:6-7, 11-12). He had abdicated, expecting the three friends of Job, and Job himself, to affirm the fact that God was still in charge even in the face of uncertainty.

Those who abdicate can identify with Elihu's statement: "Inside I am like bottled-up wine, like new wineskins ready to burst" (Job 32:19). Any staff person who has listened to a verbal pastor talk incessantly has felt like Elihu. The staff person abdicates because the pastor is the leader, but he has much to say. He or she just has not had the opportunity.

Evading.—"He who loves a quarrel loves sin" (Prov. 17:19). There is a time to be evasive. There is a time to abdicate.

Church members who delight in baiting a minister know how to turn on the faucets of opinion. "What do you think about the controversy going on in the Southern Baptist Convention?" These persons have a never-ending supply of hot items to discuss.

An overaggressive person will agree that "silence may be golden, but sometimes it is simply yellow." On occasion, there is wisdom in abdication. Silence may be the better part of wisdom.

Compromising.—Rudyard Kipling is credited with saying, "Both triumph and defeat are imposters." Some believe "being right" is not enough. These people need to convince others to change their minds and agree with them. They must defeat someone before they feel the taste of triumph.

Recently, a church member called our LeaderCare hotline to complain about his pastor. "How does the Southern Baptist Convention correct bad doctrine in pastors?" He had a list of doctrinal heresies. His pastor was guilty of preaching that people could be forgiven of any sin, even adultery. This, he said, was obviously heresy. The solution, he felt, was to terminate the pastor.

After we talked, he shared a deeper level of concern. The minister of education had had an affair with his wife. They had been in therapy, but his wife had decided divorce was the only solution. He had gone to the chairman of deacons to demand that he talk to the pastor and terminate the minister of education. The chairman of deacons discussed the possibility that the affair could have been platonic. Several complications made the situation difficult, but the pastor and the chairmen were trying to find a compromise consistent with Christian forgiveness and understanding. The minister of education finally resigned, but the anger in the church member lingered. He had residual feelings of being abandoned. The minister of education was not disciplined enough. He was not publicly punished. Compromise was a sign of weakness to this church member. The pastor should be terminated because of heresy. The chairman of deacons should resign.

Withdrawing.—Every communication system needs a cooling-down period when the steam gets too hot. Every leader needs to withdraw occasionally to refresh and renew effectiveness.

Surrendering.—"Giving in" is not "giving up."

"Better a patient man than a warrior, a man who controls his temper than one who takes a city" (Prov. 16:32). Some battles are better not fought. Constructive communication can be "I was wrong; you were right." One of the great memories of the Civil War was Robert E. Lee's dignity when he surrendered at Appomattox. As he rode his white horse to the courthouse, even Union soldiers saluted him. His face showed no shame, only sadness.

Surrendering in the face of adversity may be the best part of getting close to those who have stymied the work of the church.

Empowering, parenting, reacting, and abdicating are four patterns of communication. Some are more effective than others. All can be adopted as patterns which lead to effectiveness.

---

[1] E. Y. Mullins, *The Axioms of Religion* (Philadelphia: American Baptist Publication Society, 1908), 210.

[2] Rex Horne, "Encouragers," *The (Little Rock) Record*, 16 September 1998.

[3] Robert K. Greenleaf, *On Becoming a Servant Leader* (San Francisco: Josey-Bass Publishers, 1996), 48.

[4] Ibid.

[5] Jay Conger, *The Charismatic Leader* (San Francisco: Josey-Bass Publishers, 1989), 114.

[6] Ibid.

[7] *Sports Illustrated*, 31 August 1998.

TIPS	
1	If you share the work, share the credit.
2	Find the right people, then turn them loose and permit them to do the job.
3	Micromanagement demotivates creative persons.
4	If people have the responsibility, they should have the authority.
5	Give people room to make mistakes, but help them correct them.
6	Carefully define the territories of responsibility, then respect them. It's great teamwork.
7	Which is better: "You goofed!" or, "We can learn from this!"?
8	Never scold a colleague in front of others; it is demeaning.
9	A covenant is more binding than a job description.
10	In delegation, look for persons who are strong in areas where you are weak. Never dump work.
11	Compulsive-obsessive behavior alienates coworkers. Look for competence not perfection.
12	Every worker looks for compassion from a manager.
13	No one is lazy except in the pursuit of someone else's goals and objectives.
14	When others have egg on their face, they don't need scorn; they need support.
15	Jesus placed His mission in the hands of others, then trusted them to do it.

Eliab did not want to do the job himself, but neither did he want his youngest brother to get the credit for taking responsibility. "When Eliab, David's oldest brother, heard him speaking with the men, he burned with anger at him and asked, 'Why have you come down here? And with whom did you leave those few sheep in the desert? I know how conceited you are and how wicked your heart is; you came down only to watch the battle'" (1 Sam. 17:28).

When a minister turns loose of a work, he may have several possible motives. If it is a job he does not want to tackle himself, for whatever reason, he may decide to leave the job undone. Eliab did not want to fight the giant; but he certainly did not want his younger, smaller, and inexperienced brother to do the job. He was his father's favorite, and he was always doing things to get attention. Eliab was fearful and unwilling to take the risk. David was bold, courageous, and gifted. He was certain to get the accolades Eliab so desperately wanted.

A prominent layman had been through the "Experiencing God" training in a state event. The minister of music had accompanied him. The two came back from the event excited about the possibilities for their own church. The layman had been impressed with the skill with which the minister of music had grasped the concept of "Experiencing God." When he suggested to the pastor that the minister of music lead the church through the appropriate training for "Experiencing God," the pastor reacted with surprising anger.

"You do not realize what that would do to my role as pastor. If he led us through this training, it would undermine my influence. I need to be identified with the spiritual training. The minister of music needs to be identified with the musical training." The layman later interpreted this to mean that the pastor was not willing to go through the rigors of training for himself, but on the other hand, he was also unwilling for anyone else to lead the training. This was especially true since the pastor used the phrase "fair-haired boy" to describe the minister of music. The pastor had been in the church 12 years. The minister of music had been in the church 18 months.

The layman interpreted the pastor's resistance as an unwillingness to have anyone do something that might diminish his influence. This pastor had many similarities to Eliab, the brother of David.

Another motive for giving your job away may be simply to establish position. Unfortunately, some tasks are deemed too menial for the pastor to handle. "I don't have time for that." How much better to say, "Give me a little time, and I will find an answer."

"That's not my job" gives the impression that the job is beneath you.

A third motive, and a more positive one, for giving your job away may be overload. Some ministers simply do not have time to do justice to all the responsibilities and expectations of their job. Sharing the load can be sharing the burden of too much to do with the time allotted. Find out what you do best and do it. Find out what others do best and empower them to do it.

The Seduction of Reluctance to Empower Others by Turning Loose

Why are some free to delegate? Why are others shackled with the burden of too much to do and not enough hours to do it? Why are some pastors and staff willing to share the credit, while others hoard it like a miser?

The reluctance to delegate is seductive. We are seduced into feeling no one can do the job as we can. We are seduced into possessing certain gifts and pretending we have many others by the sheer accolades of well-meaning church members.

Some ministers have a morbid fear of not being in the flow of "in the know." What if things are going on in this church I do not know about? What will the deacons think of me if they have more information about the church than do I?

This morning I chatted briefly with our Pastor-Staff Leadership Department director, Don Mathis, about delegation. Don has been a pastor for more than three decades, an executive director of the West Virginia Baptist Convention, and now the director of our department. "What," I asked, "is your opinion about the most essential ingredient in delegation for a pastor?"

"Two things," he said. "First, you must be willing to turn it loose and allow the other person to do it. Second, and this should be first, be sure you find the right person to do the work before you ask."

Don Mathis has not been seduced into being reluctant to delegate a task that needs to be done. He is not afraid for others to get credit for a job well done. Also, he is not afraid to have the person to whom he has delegated make a mistake.

Major Glitches in Delegating

Can't let go.—Some ministers hold on too tight. They need the feel of the grip. They want to have all the information at their fingertips. In business, this is called "micromanaging." Unfortunately, it is prevalent in some churches as well.

Fear of competition.—Ministers are human, too. The competitive juices pump even when we are not aware of this phenomenon. We want to do our best. But sometimes we compare our best with the best of others. If their plate is full, we feel we should have a fuller plate. If they work 10 hours per day, we work 12 hours per day. If they visit the hospital three times per week, we visit the hospital four times per week. If they make personal witnessing visits three times per week, we make personal witnessing visits four times per week. We get caught up in the fever pitch of overly enthusiastic preachers who say, "It is better to burn out than to rust out." I'm not sure many families of ministers would give a hearty amen to that statement.

I could do this better.—I could do this better if I just did it myself. The truth is, these ministers may be right. But it is a matter of priorities. Is this what you want to spend all your time doing? Or can someone else do it equally well if not better? Delegation becomes a selective choice for those things which may be done as a part of the job description of another staff person or even a volunteer church member. The feeling, "I could do this better," is the trap of well-intentioned ministers who feel the necessity of doing things better and faster if they do it themselves.

I could do this quicker.—Creative delegation takes time. An office associate complained in a staff retreat, with some prompting for openness, that the minister of education would delegate a job, and, if the job was not done in the time frame he expected, he would habitually say, "Just don't worry about it. I will do it." The office associate said she thought the minister of education felt he was doing her a favor. In reality, she was being insulted. He felt, so she thought, that no one could do it as quickly as he could. So he would "lift" the burden by finishing the job himself. Over a period of months, the pattern developed to the point that she felt, "No matter how quickly I do it, he will take it back and do it himself." After working with him for a few months, she offered her resignation. They worked it out and she stayed, after they negotiated the compulsive manner in which he delegated his work.

In the book *Plan or Die!* the authors compared a new idea (nurturing) to a newborn child. "Human offspring require years of feeding, clothing, supporting, educating, training, and otherwise nurturing. A newborn colt, on the other hand, is on its feet within minutes after birth and is relatively self-sufficient within days. Many people who generate notions of change unfortunately see their ideas as self-sufficient young horses, not as dependent babies."[1] Compare this idea to the minister of education who does not understand why others cannot see his idea as a self-sufficient young horse. Some view a new idea much differently—as dependent babies. That does not make the opposing view wrong; it just demands more patience. Some things take more time than others. The end result could be that it is done more efficiently. The minister of education may have done the task more quickly, but when delegated properly, the office associate may have done it more efficiently and effectively.

Some Practical Steps for More Effective Empowering of Others

Covenant together.—Working together in a Baptist church is a lot like a marriage. There should be a mutual covenant. Loving one another is not only a biblical mandate, but it also makes good sense to be able to get things done without feeling "dumped on."

A covenant assumes loyalty. One of the tragedies of the presidential scandal of 1998 was the coerced behavior of the president's personal secretary. Forced to use code names to summon the young intern to the president's office, she repeatedly protected her boss. Later she was brought before the grand jury where she revealed the plots of the two persons involved. She was dumped on and was expected to show blind loyalty.

When immorality is self-evident, the covenant has limits. Most covenants, however, suggest loving and caring loyalty. I called a pastor recently. The receptionist/office associate was evasive about the whereabouts of the pastor. The urgency of the call was evident to the associate. Finally, she responded: "I never know where he is. He is in. He is out. He never tells us anything about his goings and comings."

Although understandably frustrated, loyalty might have suggested that the associate be a bit more diplomatic: "He is away from his office at the moment. May I try to get in touch with him and have him return your call?" That would be loyalty. It would also be much more professional.

Consider where others are strongest.—Delegation—that is,

proper and appropriate delegation—is a gift. Delegation is keying into the gifts and strengths of others. In the Old Testament is a verse that foreshadows the passage about Jesus' childhood in the New Testament. The Old Testament passage is about Samuel: "And the boy Samuel continued to grow in stature and in favor with the LORD and with men" (1 Sam. 2:26). By the revelation of God, the author appraised the gifts of Samuel.

In the New Testament, a similar passage is in Luke 2:40: "And the child grew and became strong; he was filled with wisdom, and the grace of God was upon him." Luke, being a physician, was sensitive to this potential for growth, both physical and spiritual.

Proper and appropriate delegation is a gift. It is a gift many are blessed to claim. But it is also a gift that can be developed. It takes a healthy self-concept and a faith that is strong enough to give others credit.

Jim Henry, pastor of First Baptist Church, Orlando, Florida, once told a pastor's conference in Kentucky that he looked for staff persons who were more gifted in their assignment than was he.[2] The gift of finding the right person for the right work is no small task. It is a hard and laborious task, but it can be eased with the leadership of the Holy Spirit. Finding the right persons for the right jobs can lead to years of covenant relationships. Finding the wrong person can be a nightmare.

Prayerful consideration should be given by the church and the potential person being considered for a specific job. If the person being selected is a paid staff person, several precautions should be taken:

✔ Person-to-person interviews with potential coworkers.
✔ Transcripts, when possible, from colleges and seminaries.

✔ Look for competence not perfection. It is impossible to satisfy all the wants and needs of church members for any staff position.

✔ References should be checked out carefully and comprehensively. Try to avoid getting caught up in the overzealous religious language of those who support the potential staff person. For example, "He is God's man. I know it."

✔ Don't be afraid to seek out financial accountability history. Although somewhat awkward in gathering the information, churches have avoided numerous problems by being careful early. You may need to get some help from legitimate businesspersons in gathering this information.

✔ Look for and expect churchmanship. Giving records, attendance, support of other staff persons' responsibilities help determine whether the candidate is a team player.

✔ When appropriate, use leadership instruments which inventory ministry and leadership gifts. Use competent and credentialed persons to interpret these, and limit access to the information.

✔ Pray about it. Ask responsible leaders in the church to pray about it.

God has a way of leaving His fingerprints where we least expect them.

Develop understanding.—Make sure what is delegated is fully understood. A job description can be helpful, but a mutual covenant based on a person's word is even more substantial. In the Old Testament a covenant was called a "RIV." It was a legal document which the Hebrews drew up out of lack of trust. But Jeremiah called for a new kind of "RIV" in Jeremiah 31:31-34. Where previously, the RIV was written on stone, or tablets, this new covenant was written on people's hearts. It was a reaffirmation of the value of "giving your word." When we reach understandings with persons who have been delegated a responsibility, we should have it written on our hearts, and it should be fully understood.

Trust the person to get the job done.—While writing this portion of *Getting on Top of Your Work*, I talked with Dr. Michael Smith, pastor, Second Baptist Church, Memphis, Tennessee, about what he thought was the most essential ingredient for delegating in a Baptist church. Without a moment's hesitation, he said, "Trust." Then he added, "I would add a descriptive adjective: *intentional* trust."

When pressed on what that meant, he said, "Trust is not automatic. It is not for the naive." You must decide to trust persons to whom you delegate, or they will feel you are taking it away from them even after you have given it to them.

When trust is sensed and felt, the pattern is to feel the freedom to try new things. If mistakes are made, they will be corrected. It is not as if their job was on the line. The area of freedom enhances the initiative of creative and exceptional work. Jesus empowered His disciples. They made many mistakes. He still loved them. Can we do any less?

Don't ever give up.—I have an overhead cell of a pelican and a frog. The pelican has swallowed the head of the frog. The frog's front legs are shaped in the cartoon fashion of arms and hands. He is holding onto the neck of the pelican. It is impossible for the pelican to swallow while being choked. The caption of the cartoon is, "Don't ever give up."

Nothing can replace persistence and tenacity in delegation. The pastor must believe in the person to whom something has been delegated. Obstinate and difficult staff members sometimes tempt pastors to concede to the barkings of church members. It is

Don't Ever Give Up!

easier to stay in good graces with church members by siding with the church member instead of the church staff member. When delegation is given, those with integrity practice persistence and tenacity in allowing the freedom to get the job done—even in the face of adversity.

After working for more than 30 years with pastors and staff persons who have been terminated, I have developed a few prejudices. Most directors of missions do their best to salvage the relationships of pastors and churches who have reached an overwhelming impasse. A few however, use the Pilate syndrome, and wash their hands of the entire episode. Their reasons vary. I am not so presumptuous as to believe that the director of missions delegates any responsibility to either the pastor or the church. I do believe he has a spiritual responsibility of delegating the need to resolve a relationship between the pastor and church which has reached ballistic dimensions.

He can stay visible.

He can let the pastor and responsible members of the church know that he is praying for their decision-making processes.

He can offer his services as mediator.

He can give his utmost attention to helping by offering the resources of the association. Thankfully, most do. Some, however, need some encouragement to be more persistent and tenacious in delegating the love and compassion of Christ. It could save a ruptured relationship.

If all else fails.—Admittedly, delegation sometimes fails. At this time we need all the biblical guidance possible. Paul had a rift with John Mark. Later, he had a rift with Barnabas. Then in the church at Antioch, Paul opposed Peter because, Paul said, "he was clearly in the wrong" (Gal. 2:11).

In chapter 3, we discussed some of the people who are hard to get along with and ultimately some who are resistant to delegated work. The New Testament pattern of reconciliation should be followed, but those persons who are too emotionally disturbed to work out the difficulties demand more dramatic actions. If staff members are unmotivated and/or have too many professional interests and investments of their energy to give to their work, this too demands more dramatic actions.

When this occurs, responsible persons should:
1. Decide to act.
2. Evaluate the working conditions, and place remedial actions in the responsibilities of the person.

3. Involve leaders who relate to this person.

4. Work out a timetable for reconciliation.

5. Work out options if the actions are not taken to work out reconciliation.

6. When all else fails, take action.

7. Do not give up on the person, but help the person get located in a place where he or she is more fulfilled.

I have been a fan of the acting abilities of Charles Grodin for several years. He is now a narrator for NBC cable out of Los Angeles. He played the husband of Goldie Hahn in the comedy *Seems Like Old Times,* which also starred Chevy Chase. When the movie first came out, he made several talk-show appearances to promote the movie. This ultimately led to his serving as host to the late-night cable show on NBC. In an interview with David Letterman, he was asked about his penchant for playing second-fiddle parts, or supporting roles. He said, "I've always had a gift for recognizing the gifts of others, then using my support gifts to make them look good."

That would be a great format for pastors in effectively empowering others. Jesus said, "Be careful not to do your 'acts of righteousness' before men, to be seen by them" (Matt. 6:1). We could learn to support our colleagues so that acts of righteousness would not be focused on ourselves. Delegation may be as simple as helping others to do their work effectively and to look good in the process.

---

[1] Timothy N. Nolan, Leonard D. Goodstein, and J. William Pfeiffer, *Plan or Die! 10 Keys to Organizational Success* (Amsterdam: Pfeiffer and Company, 1993), 95.

[2] Jim Henry, in a pastors' conference in Owensboro, Kentucky, 1986.

MAKING TIME FOR THE IMPORTANT THINGS

TIPS

1. Make a list of priorities for tomorrow at the end of every day. Then forget them until tomorrow.

2. Ministers, more than most, need to learn the fine art of saying no— but saying it gracefully.

3. Define your limits of time on the telephone. People are more understanding than we think.

4. "There is a time for everything" (Eccl. 3:1).

5. Allow yourself the luxury of chunks of time, even spontaneous visits. But define the limits to yourself and others.

6. If the communication requires a personal touch, use the telephone.

7. If the communication requires getting a job done, use e-mail.

8. If the communication requires a major decision, make a personal visit.

9. Be purposive with time; it's stress reducing.

10. Maximize your prime-time energy by concentrating on complex tasks.

11. Listen to your body; it will tell you when it is time to rest.

12. Know the difference between shooting the breeze and planning your work.

13. Pace yourself. God does not expect of us more than we can do.

14. Don't allow yourself to be swamped by details which become drudgery.

15. Group similar tasks.

16. Don't expect more of yourself than you can do.

"There is a right time for everything" (Eccl. 3:1, TLB).

"Don't be fools; be wise; make the most of every opportunity you have for doing good" (Eph. 5:16, TLB).

One of the saddest commentaries on the role of a pastor was made by a pastor: "Pastors don't have close friends; they have church members." We all know what he means. We all agree in a sense. But it should not be. We have to make time for friends.

A satirist wrote, "Friends come and go; enemies accumulate." If that is true, and sometimes I agree, we have a linear sense of timing in being sure we make and keep good friends. Friends, and making friends, is part of scheduling our time as ministers.

I am going to stick my neck out a little further. Making friends takes the pressure off a lot of prickly issues in the ministry. If we have genuine friends, we will be able to withstand the wiles of the devil. We will be able to deal with the pressures that so easily beset us. But without friends, we are in a pickle. Why?

Friends have a way of giving back to us. Most all other activities drain our energies. Even the good we do will drain us. Jesus spent much of His time recuperating. Can we expect less of ourselves? Poor scheduling has much to do with making and keeping friends. Friends have been a resource to my energy reserve. Enemies and those on the borderline of being friends suck us dry.

You cannot schedule intelligently until you have scheduled making and keeping friends into your life. I include in that category the first level of friendship, your spouse and children.

On more than one occasion, Jimmy Draper has said, "My best friend is Carole Ann" (his wife). My best friend is my wife, Shirley Anne. In spite of the fact that we have gone through 45 years of adjustments and sometimes adversity, she remains my best friend. In my early years as a consultant for the Sunday School Board (now LifeWay Christian Resources of the Southern Baptist Convention), I thought my first priority was my job. As a pastor, I thought my first priority was my church. I was wrong on both counts. My first priority beyond commitment to my Lord is my wife and family. Many ministers and wives could solve most of their problems if they would schedule more time for each other. It should be mandated. When Paul was discussing the role of the minister, he quickly established this foundation: "If anyone sets his heart on being an overseer, he desires a noble task. Now the overseer must be above reproach, the husband of but one wife" (1 Tim. 3:1-2). The family issue is first. He must be above reproach; then he begins to deal with the family issue. The minister must make time for the spouse. This relationship is critical to establishing any other priorities in ministry.

In the New Testament, two Greek words—*kairos* and *chronos*—are used for the word *time*. *Kairos* means a fixed time or a time fulfilled. *Chronos* means a more informal period or a time filled full. *Kairos* is used in Matthew 12:1, "At that time Jesus went through the grainfields on the Sabbath. His disciples were hungry." *Chronos* is used in Luke 1:57, "Now the time came for Elizabeth to be delivered" (RSV). *Chronos* was used here because this time for Elizabeth was a period of rejoicing, a time "filled full."

Most of us are much better at *kairos* than with *chronos*. I don't think Jesus had a pocket calendar, do you? He was aware of the responsibility of time, but His "hanging out" time was more important to Him than "getting things done." This does not diminish the necessity to "get things done." We must. But it does put a priority on scheduling. Jesus walked long distances to "hang out" with friends Lazarus, Mary, and Martha. He spent considerable time with His disciples talking about heavenly things. It was not so much a theological issue. It was an eternal issue of being with people whose company He enjoyed.

A Pretest for Making Time for the Important Things

Here is a little exercise I often use in working with ministers and spouses to assess spiritual influences on their relationships. It works for scheduling time as well. It was developed by P. Pruyser in *The Minister as Diagnostician* and summarized in the American Association of Christian Counselors journal, *Marriage and Family*.

The Seven Categories for Pastoral Diagnosis
1. What do you hold most sacred in your life?
2. On a scale from 1 to 10, where would you place trust and hope in your life?
3. To what have you committed yourself?
4. For what are you most thankful, been given, been forgiven for, or been forgiving?
5. What sin in your life has not been dealt with? (Separate conversations with couples.)
6. With whom do you reach out, care for, and feel cared for?
7. Describe the sense of satisfaction and purpose you find in your life and work.[1]

Take time to write the answers to these questions before you look seriously at scheduling your time in your life and ministry.

Prime-Time Performers

Some ministers appear to accomplish mountains of activities and events and still maintain a sunny disposition. Others appear to accomplish a smidgen in comparison and are always disgruntled. Why? One of America's top authorities on successful time management and personal productivity thinks she has the answer. High achievers have mastered techniques that simplify their lives and make work more efficient. Stephanie Winston's popular books have sold more than a million copies. They are *Getting Organized* and *The Organized Executive*. Her answer: "prime time" work. Work when you have energy levels at maximum height and speed.[2]

Every person has different levels of prime-time energy. Barry Goheen is still a mystery to me. Barry was a guard with the Vanderbilt Commodore basketball team in the late '80s and early '90s. Vanderbilt had a reasonably good team and went to the "Sweet 16" of the NCAA basketball tournament Barry's junior year. The mystery of this good team was that it was great during the last two minutes of most games when Barry Goheen became an athletic animal. Eight times during his career, he had buzzer beaters to win the game. The most significant was against Pittsburgh to put Vanderbilt in the "Sweet 16." He hit a three-point goal with 23 seconds to go, then another with 1 second to go to erase a 6-point deficit. Overtime. Then he hit another and another. He made only16 points that game, but 15 of them were made from the 23-second point through overtime. Vanderbilt won.

He was not an exceptional scorer—approximately 12.5 points per game—but during the last two minutes he was phenomenal. Some superstars fall apart during crunch time. Barry was a "prime timer' during the last two minutes. For months ESPN ran an excerpt on this phenomenal player.

Everyone has peak or prime times in productivity. Find yours, and you can join the list of high achievers.

Compelled or Propelled

Consider two kinds of leaders. The first feels compelled to spend time "doing things," while the second is propelled to "get things done." A leader in a large company with more than 1,500 persons looked out his office window to be sure everyone was at work on time. After observing some chronic latecomers, he had the doors locked so that employees would be counted absent because they were late. For a few days, employees felt demoralized. But then recognizing the absurdity of the restriction, many began playing games to frustrate. Cartoons drawn by creative mavericks were placed in conspicuous places. The restriction was soon lifted.

Another compulsion is the "hall monitor." This is the person who feels compelled to walk through the offices to monitor those who say they arrive at six-thirty, a flex-time arrangement. Then the activity is repeated in the afternoon after three. I know a pastor who records a time card for the entire staff.

There are more effective ways to monitor time than to have persons feel compelled to be there.

The more effective way is the propelled group. This group is excited about their work. They know they have a job to do. They feel they are trusted to do the job, and most of these people work far beyond expectations simply because they love it.

Winston called this technique "leveraging." These employees rapidly process and filter vast amounts of information. They know how to decide on priorities. They get things done. But more importantly, they have what she called a "compulsion to closure."[3] They live by periods rather than commas. Things come to a close. Isn't it exhausting to be around persons who make the same decisions over and over? Isn't it exhausting to be around people who have a compulsion for persons to be at a place simply because they need an audience? Some time-management experts have called this a need for a "palace guard." They are so regal in their own thinking that they must have a palace guard to do their bidding.

Those who are propelled into their time-saving techniques are those who are motivated from within. After all, no one is lazy except in the pursuit of someone else's goals or ideals.

Make Time for the Important Things in Life

Simplify.—Don't make simple things complicated. Know the difference between shooting the breeze and planning your work. If you plan a meeting for one hour, honor it. It shows respect for others, but it also shows respect for your own needs. Some pastors stand while communicating with others in the office. This allows them to get to the point without abusing anyone's time.

List your priority activities for the next day before you complete the day. Start with the toughest activities and work down.

Group similar tasks.—A minister of education recently suggested to other conference participants that the hardest part of his work was impromptu staff meetings called by the pastor. He said these often took place several times per day. The pastor's schedule took precedence over any tasks. The pastor could save himself a lot of grief by grouping similar tasks and planning a staff meeting in advance. A herky-jerky modus operandi suggests this pastor has not thought through his agenda. Treating people this way is demeaning. It shows a lack of respect for those with whom he works.

Telephones/e-mail.—Communication in a church is our job. Telephones keep us in contact with the people we serve. But time-saving telephone techniques can alleviate enormous stress.

> *Pastor John (to administrative associate):* Get Bob on the phone.
>
> *Administrative Associate:* Brother Bob, please. Yes, I'll wait.
>
> *(Feeling the urgency of the call from the pastor, Brother Bob is asked to leave a conference with a client.)*
>
> *Brother Bob:* Hello, Yes, this is Bob.
>
> *Administrative Associate:* Will you please hold for the pastor?
>
> *Three minutes later, after the pastor has had a brief conversation with a drop-in visitor, the administrative associate has finally been able to transfer the call:* I have Brother Bob on the phone.
>
> *Pastor John:* Ask him to hold a minutes.
>
> *Administrative Associate:* Brother Bob, could you hold a minute?
>
> *A frustrated Brother Bob patiently waits for the pastor to connect.*

Could this activity be done more efficiently and more effectively? Yes, I think so. The pastor could have dialed directly. He would have saved himself, the administrative associate, and Brother Bob a lot of time. Time-saving techniques are for everyone.

The idea that one person's time is more important than another's is insulting and demeaning.

Counseling on the telephone is an important part of pastoral care, but all problems cannot be solved at one time. A minister must decide what can be done on the phone and what cannot be done on the phone. Key phrases must be learned and practiced:

- "This matter needs more thought."
- "We need to discuss this with _____. Please set up a time for the three of us to talk this over."
- "This is a serious problem and would be embarrassing if she found out we were discussing it. Why don't we work on a way to get her involved in helping us solve this problem?"

All of these key phrases place the responsibility back on the caller. Asking the caller to be accountable for the discussion topic has a way of drawing to a conclusion a never-ending conversation.

You may want to use these techniques for saving time,

- Before reaching for the telephone, ask yourself if E-mail would suffice?
- Is this the best way to complete this task?
- Before you call, list items that need to be covered?
- Learn to say, without guilt and with diplomacy, "Please forgive me. I have an appointment." Even if the appointment is another activity, it is still an appointment.
- Call when you are sure you can reach your party.
- Set a time when you can regularly accept calls.
- Screen your calls. If what you are doing is more important than accepting the call, stick to what you are doing.
- If you are in conference, honor the conferee by refusing to accept the call unless it is an emergency.
- If you work through a secretary in accepting calls, give a list of those with whom you must speak when they call,

as well as a list of those who can be referred. Every church has a few chronic callers. These persons may need to talk because of their loneliness or boredom. Every intelligent staff person learns who these persons are and works out a caring response which will minimize the use of the minister's time.

Time-saving resources.

Toolbox for Busy Pastors, Barry Campbell (Nashville: Convention Press, 1998). This book can save you hours, days of time. It is prepared to give you a ready reference for practical answers to everyday questions in the ministry. Look at some of the chapters (which will save you time):

- How to Develop Purpose and Vision Statements for Your Church
- How to Deal with Ineffective Workers
- How to Develop an Annual Preaching Plan
- How to Conduct a Funeral Service
- How to Prepare for a Wedding
- How to Ordain a Minister
- How to Exercise
- How to Overcome Discouragement
- How to Care for Persons in Crisis
- How to Teach Lifestyle Stewardship
- How to Find and Enlist a Staff Member
- How to Publish a Great Newsletter
- How to Make a Visit

The list goes on, with 100 topics. Pick up a copy at a LifeWay Christian Bookstore, or order one by calling 1-800-458-2772.

Surviving and Thriving in the Ministry, Don Mathis (Nashville: Convention, 1997). Not only a "get by" but a "thriving" approach to dealing with ministry.

Building Blocks for Longer Life and Ministry, Tommy Yessick (Nashville: Convention, 1997). A healthy lifestyle may save your life—emotionally, intellectually, spiritually, and physically. You need this on your desk. It will save you hours of time in building a healthy lifestyle for effective ministry.

The People of God: Essays on the Believers' Church, ed. Paul Basden and David S. Dockery (Nashville: Broadman, 1991). This book can save you hours in answering questions often asked in a Baptist church. Essays on baptism, Lord's Supper, worship, discipline, priesthood of all believers, images of the church, role of women in the church, and contemporary challenges deal with most of the hard questions asked by serious students of God's Word and Baptist history. It will save you time.

Holman Bible Dictionary, ed. Trent Butler (Nashville: Broadman, 1991). This dictionary has a definition of just about any name or word discussed in a Baptist church. It's expensive, but it will pay for itself in time saved.

The Complete Biblical Library (Springfield, MO: Complete Biblical Library, 1989). Each volume has a word-by-word interpretation of the original language. Although the Old Testament is currently incomplete, this set of commentaries, though relatively expensive, will serve you in sermon preparation, teaching aids, word studies, January Bible Studies, and book studies. Serious students of the original languages of the Bible will love the thoroughness of this time-saving set of commentaries.

The Care of Troublesome People, Wayne E. Oates (Chicago: Alban Institute, 1994). The book deals with what the title suggests.

I will not insult your intelligence by suggesting that you should have several good translations of God's Word, including New International, New King James, Revised Standard, and Amplified. But a number of others will save you time in study if you find the ones with which you are compatible.

Baptist Faith and Message, Herschel H. Hobbs (Nashville: Convention, 1998).

Kingdom Principles Growth Strategies Kit, Gene Mims and Mike

Miller (Nashville: Convention, 1994). This kit will save time in developing strategies for reaching people for Christ and helping your church carry out the Great Commission.

Jesus CEO, Laurie Beth Jones (New York: Hyperion, 1992). This bestseller uses biblical wisdom for visionary leadership in a contemporary environment. Quick reading with gems of wisdom to give sparkle to your sermons. It sizzles with new ideas.

Don't Sweat the Small Stuff—and It's All Small Stuff, Richard Carlson (New York: Hyperion, 1997). Simple ways to keep little things in perspective and to keep them from taking over your life.

Preaching with Spiritual Passion, Ed Rowell (Minneapolis: Bethany, 1998). How to keep the pizzazz in your preaching.

Kingdom Leadership, Michael Miller (Nashville: Convention, 1996).

These are but a few of the books that will save you time and energy in your search for compartmentalizing your priorities in order to have time for the important things in life.

The 96-to-1 Ratio Theory

24 Hours

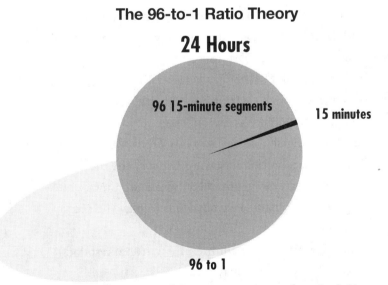

96 15-minute segments

15 minutes

96 to 1

The ratio is 96 to 1. The following is a theory for scheduling as a matter of making time for the important things in life.

Although I am not a fan of Andy Warhol, many people are. He is perhaps more famous for obscure and modernistic art than for his verbal exploits. More than one speaker has credited him with the statement, "Within every person's life, they will have 15 minutes." Interpreted, it means, every person will have some semblance of fame, recognition, notoriety, contribution, or visibility for a brief period. It lasts only a moment. At best, 15 minutes. A small amount of time compared to a life of 80 or more years.

Suppose our lives were divided into 15-minute segments. Even more focused, suppose our lives were divided into one day with 96 segments. Each 24-hour day has 96 separate segments.

Everything may be centered on that 15 minutes. Mary Lou Retton, in the course of three days in 1984, accomplished with memorable charisma what no other human being has been able to accomplish in gymnastics. She won the gold as the all-around gymnastics champion. She had her 15 minutes.

In September 1998, Mark McGwire went where no man has ever been in baseball. He demolished Roger Maris' record of 61 home runs, by hitting 70 home runs; and the pennant races, playoffs, and World Series paled in the shadow of this remarkable feat. Mark McGwire had his 15 minutes.

In June 1998, Michael Jordan and the Chicago Bulls had their 15 minutes with their fifth world title. The Boston Celtics had their 15 minutes with 9 world titles.

Earl Nightingale told this story in *The Winner's Circle*:

> At a reception following her concert, the gifted pianist was approached by an admirer, who gushed, "I would give anything to play the piano as you do."
>
> Looking at the admirer, the virtuoso responded, "No, you wouldn't."
>
> She now had everyone's astonished attention.
>
> The admirer was embarrassed, but pursued her

point. "But I would, too, I'd give anything to play like you."

The concert pianist smiled. "I'm not criticizing you, understand. I'm just saying you don't mean it. Because, perhaps you could play as well. But it would take 20 years of practicing, hour after hour, day after day. That's what it took me. That's why I say you wouldn't give anything to play as I do. Because you wouldn't give the time. And that is the one thing it takes to accomplish our goals—time."[4]

Those few moments of performance, compared to all the preparation and practice, are only 15 minutes.

A natural response might be, Is that all there is? We build our lives on 15 minutes? Is that what Lee Harvey Oswald wanted? 15 minutes of notoriety? or John Hinckley? or Mark David Chapman? or Squeaky Fromm? or James Earl Ray? Are these persons so desperate that they invade history with unspeakable, cruel, and evil activities? Some people appear to trade their souls for 15 minutes. There is a better way.

On November 18, 1998, superstars in bestsellers in leadership and management expertise joined in leading a seminar, "Worldwide Lessons in Leadership Series," sponsored by Vanderbilt University's Owen Graduate School of Management in cooperation with *Fortune* magazine. Ken Blanchard and Tom Peters teamed up to lead some thought-provoking topics: "How Everyone Can Build a Climate of Trust and Openness," "How to Grow Your Mental Toughness and Competence," "How to Learn from—and Earn from—Past Experience." But one in particular caught my eye: "How to Develop a Healthy Sense of Urgency." The title intrigued me because it seems to me the spirit of expectancy is the one ingredient for those who would prepare for their 15 minutes in a positive way. Too much urgency may give ulcers. Too little urgency may give the impression of apathy or laziness. But a healthy sense of urgency is the anticipation of something important and significant happening in their lives.

Philemon has only 25 verses. It is powerful but brief. Perhaps Philemon had his 15 minutes in the close relationship with Paul. But Onesimus shouts for attention. Why was Paul willing to go to the wall for Onesimus? What had he done that caused Paul to call him his "son" and to plead for reconciliation? While Paul was in chains, Onesimus had his 15 minutes in history. He had affirmed, or supported, or prayed for Paul.

I believe there is a road map for having your 15 minutes. I think it can be charted. The road map might follow this path:

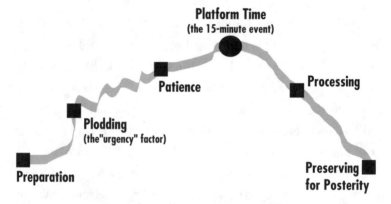

Preparation.—God calls. When He does, we should get prepared to do whatever God wants us to do. We should get prepared to become whatever God wants us to become. "Devote yourself to the public reading of Scripture, to preaching and to teaching. Do not neglect your gift" (1 Tim. 4:13-14).

Metaphorically, the 15 minutes is a small portion of your life. Preparation is also doing what God wants us to do. The anticipation of the unknown is exciting. It is a pilgrimage with God. Expectation and preparation for what we want will eventually lead to dismay and despair. Expectation and preparation for what God wants will lead us to our own 15 minutes. That 15 minutes is rarely pastoring one of the superchurches. It is rarely working in a cushy denominational job (which, by the way, does not exist). It is, on the other hand, the experience of finding what God wants out of His own purpose and discovering where we fit into His plan.

Preparation is a lifetime experience. It does not end at age 26 when we complete seminary. It begins. It is a "noble task" (1 Tim. 3:1) and demands our best.

Plodding—the urgency factor.—"So then, just as you received Christ Jesus as Lord, continue to live in him, rooted and built up in him, strengthened in the faith as you were taught, and overflowing with thankfulness" (Col. 2:6-7).

Plodding is putting first things first in ministry. It is the continuance of leading people to a saving knowledge of Jesus Christ, helping people to grow in Christ, and finding the fun of living the mind of Christ as a wonderful by-product. Plodding is the urgency factor of working until Jesus comes in the work that we were meant to do. It is having realistic expectations of ourselves. It is the ability to recognize what God has given us and continuing to sharpen and hone that gift or gifts. It is the absence of whining and complaining about our plight and being thankful as we are strengthened in the faith.

Gene Getz, in *Elijah, Remaining Steadfast Through Uncertainty*, describes how Elijah failed to get what he thought he deserved. He wanted to pastor First Baptist after his spiritual victory on Mount Carmel. What did he get? Jezebel Avenue, a nondescript church full of backbiting, terminating-minded church members led by a livid queen. (Gene would not stoop this low for a metaphor, so forgive me.) What followed was a devastating disappointment and ultimately a plea from Elijah to God: "Take my life."[5] But he survived. He plodded on and found God's counseling model in 1 Kings 19:9-18. God was not in the wind or the earthquake or the fire. Where was He? In a "gentle whisper" (v. 12). For those who plod on to find their 15 minutes, the segments leading up to it can often be measured by a gentle whisper, but it takes one willing to listen to God's encouragement even when despair is the bitter-sweet seduction.

The subtitle describes plodding: *Following God Without Looking Back.* Elijah paid the price, but he stayed the course.

Patience.—Getz suggested, "To overcome depression, we must understand and face reality."[6] That best describes patience. Paul wrote, "As God's chosen people, holy and dearly loved, clothe yourselves with compassion, kindness, humility, gentleness and patience" (Col. 3:12). The word for *patience* in Greek, the biblical language, is *makrothumian*, a noun when literally translated means "stretch out the hot." *Makro* is the word for "encompassing or stretching out over large territories." *Thumian* is the word for "heat." *Thumian* is the word we use later for *thermos*, which protects the heat. *Makrothumian* is "stretching out the hot; avoiding bottling up the heat." That is an accurate description of patience. Patience is the willingness to wait for God to act. When you are being terminated from a church, that is difficult to do. We think we know what is best for our lives, only God knows what is best for our lives. We must wait for His whispers even when that means our wives or husbands must find new friends, our children must change schools, and our livelihood is temporarily interrupted.

During these times, it is good to remember that God is too wise to make a mistake. He is too compassionate to be cruel. And He is too mysterious to explain Himself, even though many charlatans have suggested He already has. The troubled waters have undercurrents that constantly surprise us, but the shores are always visible for the person of patient faith.

Platform time—the 15-minute event.—Finally, it comes. It feels right. It feels joyous. Finally, we get the 70th home run, the gold medal, the world championship, of our life. It is the feeling that comes when God looks down on us and say, "Well done, good and faithful servant. You have been faithful with a few things; I will put you in charge of many things. Come and share your master's happiness" (Matt. 25:21).

How can we recognize the 15 minutes when it happens? Some people never do, unfortunately. A solid marriage may be the 15 minutes we seek. A child who has found Christ. Finding the joy of fulfillment in sticking by a friend when he has jeopardized his life with a scandalous sin. A son who has responded to the call to ministry. The celebration of life at the funeral of a parent. The ability to see potential and, ultimately, accomplishment in one others have given up on. It may be a simple thing. It may be a profound happening.

But one thing is certain; it is rarely what we expected. God is always full of surprises for those who wait on His purposive actions. It is rarely going to a larger church. It is not receiving a trip to the Holy Land or a new automobile. It is not even in a raise. But it could be in the baptism of a person who has been a friend for years but has never accepted Christ until you had almost given up. It could be helping a manic-depressive find the right therapist and the right medication to treat this devastating disease. It could be in helping a beloved friend to find reconciliation with God after years of battling alcohol and drugs. It could be in having a grandchild say, "You're the best Pawpaw in the world." It is rarely what we expect—that 15 minutes, but it is always a wonderful surprise. God always has bigger things planned for us than we have for ourselves. He blesses us when we least expect it. We do not even know that we have been blessed until we reflect on it.

Discovering the joy of being a devoted husband, father, and grandfather is more satisfying than being recognized for a brief moment because of a "splendid" sermon, or a "majestic" presentation, or an "extraordinary" book. Having someone say in the presence of God and others that you were an influencing factor in leading them to Christ is better than the idea of being in the top 10 percent of salaries of pastors in the Southern Baptist Convention. Being on denominational boards, committees, and agencies leaves one thirsty. But feeling the presence of the Holy Spirit is a spring that quenches the thirst in even the worst of droughts.

Processing.—Timing to a cymbal player in a symphony is vital. Timing is essential in processing what has been done. It is the difference between those who know when their time has come and those who do not know that their time has already been.

Cal Ripkin knew. He broke the record for the longest run of uninterrupted games played in major league baseball and continued the streak until the last week of 1998, when he told his manager, "It is time." He sat out a game and ended his streak. What baseball fan will ever forget Cal Ripkin Jr.'s run around the fence in the Baltimore Orioles stadium.? It was an event in sports history. Some even say it saved baseball after the embarrassing strikes in 1994. But just as gripping was his decision to sit out a game in 1998. Timing is vital. His time had come. His time had been.

Ecclesiastes 3:1-8 (RSV) describes timing.

A time to be born . . . a time to die;
a time to plant . . . a time to pluck up;
a time to kill . . . a time to heal,
a time to break down . . . a time to build up;
a time to weep . . . a time to laugh;
a time to mourn . . . a time to dance;
a time to cast away stones . . . a time to gather stones;
a time to embrace . . . a time to refrain from embracing;
a time to seek . . . a time to lose;
a time to keep . . . a time to throw away,
a time to rend . . . a time to sew;
a time to keep silence . . . a time to speak;
a time to love . . . a time to hate;
a time for war . . . a time for peace.

It is difficult to process when the 15 minutes are happening. It is essential to process after it has happened. In the passages of life it is "passing the mantle." It is processing the celebration of life, and preparing for the new pilgrimage. That was what Paul was doing when he said, "Though outwardly we are wasting away, yet inwardly we are being renewed day by day" (2 Cor. 4:16).

In my office is a photo taken this past spring of the 1953 Holcomb Hornets, of Holcomb, Missouri. We are all 45 years older. We met for the first time in 45 years to celebrate our 27–3 record and the county and regional championships in basketball in 1953. The sweet taste of victory and the agony of defeat to the teams we "should have beaten" were relived. We remembered shots, passes, words spoken, and small events that should have been long forgotten. But they were not. We processed our team's 15 minutes and relished it with gusto.

Ministers know how to work the guilt in a congregation better than they know how to celebrate. Processing is the ability to celebrate. For years I preached from Hebrews 11. I missed the heart of the chapter. The roll call of faith was huge. But bigger still was Hebrews 11:39. It was the "processing" phase of the roll call of faith: "These were all commended for their faith, yet *none of them received what had been promised. God had planned something better*" (Heb. 11:39, italics mine). The processing of the 15 minutes gives us an opportunity to reflect on how God has worked in our lives. We plan what we think God wants from us, but God always has something better planned for us.

The most disappointing events in ministry are most often the prelude to the aria which God has composed for us. We think the unfinished product of the prelude is the story. God is laying the foundation for something far better.

Processing is learning from our mistakes. Jesus said, "I came that they may have life, and have it abundantly" (John 10:10, RSV). Abundant life is not the 15 minutes. Abundant life is the processing time when we reflect on what God has done in our life, and stand in the presence of holiness, and recognize what it has been. It rarely is recognized during the time it occurs. John Savage discussed this phenomenon in *Listening and Caring Skills in Ministry, a Guide for Pastors, Counselors, and Small Group Leaders:* "It is internal convictions that help shape the way we see and understand God."[7] These internal convictions happen as the result of recognizing how God acts in our lives. And remember, "None of them received what had been promised. God had planned something better."

Preserving for posterity.—Almost a half a century ago, J. W. Storer wrote a marvelous work, *The Preacher: His Belief and Behavior.* He concluded his book with a description of the tenure of the minister. He quotes from a poem which is relevant to our last step in the 96-to-1 ratio theory:

> The years die not.
> They live and stronger grow.
> Time's finger traces deep a line to show,
> So witless men may surely know,
> The years die not.
>
> The years die not,
> Or else our labor all is vain.
> Our moment's triumph or our steady pain
> Leaves a golden priceless gain, because
> the years die not.
>
> The years die not.
> Linked are we to deathless things.
> Each growing moment with it brings
> Abiding increment on its immortal wings,
> The years die not.
> The years die not.
> Then humbly let me write upon the scroll,
> The wondrous parchment of my soul,

'To please my God, my only goal.'
The years die not.

The years die not.
Help me, dear Lord, to see,
Tho' passing swift the years may be,
When comes Thy final call for me,
The years die not! [8]

When all is said and done, hopefully more will be done than said. But it is so difficult for the minister who is a "talker" by profession. Preserving the posterity of a life is in the hands of those around us. Fifteen minutes will be what we are remembered by in posterity. Few will recall the 95. The years die not, but the memory of our 15 minutes will linger if we stay in the will of God.

Shakespeare wrote, and Storer quoted in his final chapter on "Tenure," "All the world's a stage, and all the men and women merely players. They have their exits and their entrances; and one man in his time plays many parts."[9] Preserve the exits and entrances.

I had gone through a particularly difficult time physically. Two bleeding ulcers were activated at (not by) the Southern Baptist Convention in 1997, in Dallas, Texas. It took nine units of blood to get my body functioning; but after several days in critical care, I stabilized. Then the bad news: bypass surgery was necessary because of blocked arteries. Four bypasses later, I thought I was on the mend. But a kidney stone and gall bladder removal later, I finally realized life is precious but fragile. The prayers and support of many pastors, staff, and denominational persons helped me recognize how important friends and family are. One of the most amusing incidents came as our president, Dr. Jimmy Draper, called (he was also there with my wife and family during the operation). He said, "How are you, Brooks?"

Trying to milk the moment to its ultimate and exaggerating the weakness in my voice (although not by much) I whispered, "Thanks for calling, Jimmy, but I am still pretty weak."

He replied, in a rather presidential tone, "Don't you die. We need you."

Quickly falling into my complicity role, I said, "Okay." And I didn't. But of course, eventually, I will. It was not so much a miracle because it was simply a postponement. The real miracle is death, which is the doorway to eternal life.

Miracles which postpone death are not what preserve the 15 minutes for posterity. The miracle of eternal life is the preservation for God's magnificent posterity.

Scheduling is making time for the important things in life. It is arranging your life so that it is manageable. It is maximizing the little things that would be blown away if not for a prearranged value system established with God's grace.

To that frustrated pastor who said, "I don't have time for anything anymore," I want to say: "Yes, you do. You have time for everything that you want to do. But you will never have time for the things you feel compelled to do. Compulsion is the demon of time management. Give yourself a break, and don't sweat the small stuff."

---

[1] P. Pruyser, *The Minister as Diagnostician* (Philadelphia: Westminster Press, 1977), as summarized in *Marriage and Family, a Christian Journal*, 1:3 (1998): 265.

[2] Stephanie Winston, "How America's Most Successful Executives Accomplish So Much in So Little Time," *Executive Focus*, September 1998: 23.

[3] Ibid.

[4] Earl Nightingale, from *The Essence of Success* (Niles, IL: Nightingale-Conant Corp.), as quoted in *The Winner's Circle*, September 1998.

[5] Gene Getz, *Elijah, Remaining Steadfast Through Uncertainty* (Nashville: Broadman & Holman, 1995), 133.

[6] Ibid., 150.

[7] John Savage, *Listening and Caring Skills in Ministry, a Guide for Pastors, Counselors, and Small Group Leaders* (Nashville: Abingdon, 1996), 135.

[8] J. W. Storer, *The Preacher: His Belief and Behavior* (Nashville: Broadman, 1953), 103–104.

[9] Shakespeare, *As You Like It,* act 2, scene 7, line 139.

GROWING WITH GRACE

TIPS	
1	Learning is forever. God is still painting the picture with your life.
2	Jesus modeled learning by listening to others.
3	Victories are temporary; adversity teaches us lessons for life.
4	Learning is anticipating the unexpected.
5	Every motor needs fine tuning. Learning keeps us humming.
6	If you seek wisdom from God, He will give it.
7	Pray without ceasing.
8	Everyone can teach us something.
9	If you don't know where you are going, you will end up someplace else.
10	Formalize learning. Plan sabbaticals, seminars, conferences, and learning activities which help in structured ways.
11	Physical exercise is using muscles and cells which otherwise atrophy.
12	Learning does not fear "Why?" or "Why not?"
13	Learning can be great fun.
14	The number one recreation for senior adults is learning.
15	Be accountable to someone for progress in learning.

"Let us acknowledge the Lord; let us press on to acknowledge him. As surely as the sun rises, he will appear" (Hos. 6:3).

Learning is a lifelong adventure. Improving the gifts which God has given is a lifetime experience. Getting on top of your work is a daily event. Learning is fun.

Learning is an attitude. It is a way of life.

I ran across a book in 1997 that changed much of my thinking about learning. The book, *Safe Places*, discusses "experiencing inner calm" as a way of developing a perception about past experience, which puts us in a frame of mind to learn and grow. "Some people walk through, survive, or persist in what appear to others to be impossible or unbearable situations and never seem to falter. They are not in denial. They aren't trying to win public acclaim as heroes or heroines. They aren't masochistic or suicidal. Rather, they truly have a deep, inner assurance that no matter what happens to them or around them, they are going to be okay."[1]

The authors continue, "Most people with this inner calm have faith—-faith that God is, that He cares for them, that He has a purpose and plan for their lives that will be accomplished if they yield to it and work for it, and that when their time comes to die, they immediately will embark upon an everlasting life in an eternal home."[2] This is an enviable attitude for a minister who wishes to continue his life learning.

Learning is forever. A grandfather learns from grandchildren. A wife learns from a husband. A sister learns from a brother. If learning stops, lethargy and apathy begin. Boring or adversarial relationships begin. I believe the moment we begin to assume the role of teacher and not student we begin to die intellectually. I have learned more from learners than I have learned from teachers. Those who want to teach and not learn give few signals of wanting to grow. On the other hand, those who are learners stretch us to become better than we thought we could be.

Jesus was a teacher. But even in His teaching, He was a learner. He helped persons find answers more than He gave answers. He lifted people up into the arena of discovery. He used the Socratic method of question and answer. Yes, He taught in the Sermon on the Mount, but He talked with Nicodemus. He even called Nicodemus a teacher (John 3:10). He talked with His disciples.

He questioned the Samaritan woman. He sat down at the well, but He drew more than water from the well, for He was there to draw the truth from one who was hiding from the world. He was a teacher; He helped people learn.

Learning Is Preparing for the Unexpected

Ministers who are devastated by crisis are not prepared for the unexpected. The five rules of whitewater rafting offer an excellent metaphor for survival rules in a Baptist church. They also provide a lesson in preparing for the unexpected:

1. Go with the flow and don't get addled.
2. Lean into the rocks. Rocks are your friends.
3. Feet first, toes out when you go into the turbulence.
4. If worse comes to worst, let go of everything and eventually you will come up.
5. You're here because of the danger so enjoy it.

Arterburn, Minirth, and Meier wrote, "In addition to faith, those who are prepared for potentially unsafe situations generally are able to cope with them better and emerge from them successfully." [3]

Forced termination is one of the most painful events in the minister's life. But it can be a great teacher. When a wife is in an abusive relationship with a husband, both need help. If the husband does not "learn" from the request to seek help, the wife must take dramatic actions. Sometimes the only possible solution available is to set down ultimatums. Threats from the wife are viewed as a strategy for healing the relationship. Of course, they may be seen as manipulation. In that case no one learns. But if there is a concerted effort to correct the abusive behavior, then everyone learns. Some churches can be abusive. If a minister gets into an abusive relationship with a church to the point of termination, he must learn. It has many of the same ingredients as a divorce.

A pastor went to a church that had forced the previous two

ministers to resign. "This time it will be different," he reasoned.

It began innocently enough. A young woman with her family greeted the pastor after a worship service. "I really don't think you should quote from Carl Jung."

Stunned, the pastor asked, "Why?"

"He was not a Christian. I don't want my children hearing someone who is not a Christian quoted from the pulpit." If he struggled, he could make sense of that.

A few weeks later, the chairman of deacons asked for an appointment. "Pastor, it grieves me, but I represent the deacons when I say that we don't want you using humor in the pulpit. It is degrading and inappropriate." Perhaps the pastor had not understood the cultural mores of the church, he reasoned.

The church secretary came to him in a private moment. "Last Sunday, you told the Church Council that someone had given a gift of $5,000. You must not divulge this kind of information to anyone. I will not tell you this kind of information if you are going to share it indiscriminately."

In telling the story, he said: "I had been in churches where nitpicking was seen on occasion. But this was almost epidemic. They wanted to legislate everything I said or did. I began to understand the mentality behind why the last two pastors had been terminated. They obviously resisted the legislation. Some kind of pattern had been established that gave the church a license to abuse, or legislate, or direct the actions, behavior, and words of the pastor."

What happened?

"Obviously, I could not get into a marriage counseling relationship with anyone about the church. So I divorced the church before they terminated me."

Drastic, but understandable.

Patrick Henry made one of the most famous speeches of the revolutionary era on March 23, 1775. He is remembered for the final line of the speech: "Give me liberty, or give me death." But, prior to that immortal line is one of the most invigorating pleas for strength and determination in the annals of American history. It can be captured in spirit for the incentive to grow. "If we make a proper use of those means which the God of nature hath placed in our power we are not weak. . . . We shall not fight our battles alone. There is a just God who presides over the destinies of nations, and who will raise up friends to fight our battles for us. The battle, sir, is not to the strong alone; it is to the vigilant, the active, the brave."[4]

Growth in ministry is to the vigilant, the active, the brave. Our gifts were not given and then abandoned. Our gifts were given and continue to be fine tuned by those who are the vigilant, the active, and the brave.

Improving is a lifelong experience. Paul knew it. "Not that I have already obtained all this, or have already been made perfect, but I press on to take hold of that for which Christ Jesus took hold of me. Brothers, I do not consider myself yet to have taken hold of it. But one thing I do: Forgetting what is behind and straining toward what is ahead, I press on toward the goal to win the prize for which God has called me heavenward in Christ Jesus" (Phil. 3:12-14).

I attended a seminar with the father of pastoral care in Baptist life, Dr. Wayne Oates. Just about every facet of my concept of pastoral care was taught by or inspired by Dr. Oates. When I led a conference on pastoral care, he attended. I stammered. I stuttered. I was confused. I was definitely intimidated. This was my hero.

To add to my anxiety, he was taking notes. Maybe he is preparing for the next conference. Maybe he is simply ignoring what is going on, waiting for his part on the agenda, I reasoned.

No such luck. At the luncheon, we sat together. "I was very interested in what you were saying about transformational faith in working with passive aggression," he said. He heard me.

"Would you mind if I use that concept?" he said

Mind? I thought. "It would be better than steak and biscuits at Ireland's. And I love steak and biscuits at Ireland's." Dr. Oates has always had a gift for affirming his students. The ultimate compliment is when he treats a student like a colleague.

Learning is preparing for the unexpected. The genius of my mentor is his lifelong learning prowess. He is constantly learning. He learns from everyone. Even me.

Be Realistic About Your Gifts While Learning

"Not that I have already obtained all this, or have already been made perfect, but I press on to take hold of that for which Christ Jesus took hold of me. Brothers, I do not consider myself yet to have taken hold of it. But one thing I do: Forgetting what is behind and straining toward what is ahead, I press on toward the goal to win the prize for which God has called me heavenward in Christ Jesus. All of us who are mature should take such a view of things" (Phil. 3:12-15). The power in that passage is in the crowning statement in verse 16, "Only let us live up to what we have already attained."

God has gifted us. Neil Knierim reasoned, "As one called by God to vocational ministry, you have been anointed by Him for this role."[5] That means God has gifted us by His anointing. We are responsible for being worthy of that gift. To do that we must continue to learn and grow. The Christian pilgrimage is passing from one passage to another. Knierim continued: "Persons who are secure in God's call to vocational ministry have a quiet confidence in their lives. . . . It is important for you to know that God has called you and that you have not simply chosen ministry as a profession. You are not working for God but with Him."[6]

Mike Miller has developed a learning process for the minister in *Kingdom Leadership*. It is appropriately called "The Leadership Path," a design for a lifelong learning experience for the minister:

The path begins with God's call.

The beginning leader.—This is the romance of leadership. Things are bright, optimistic, and ideal.

The assimilating leader.—Personal development is related to spiritual growth and maturity, "putting things together."

The building leader.—Here the minister becomes aware of the power of influence in leadership. "Fourteen years passed before Paul was recognized as a strong, influential leader."

The achieving leader.—The leader begins to receive growing recognition for leadership and ministry accomplishments. For example, "Paul and Barnabas remained in Antioch, teaching and preaching the word of the Lord, with many others" (Acts 15:35, NKJV). The achieving leader learns to integrate the lessons of leadership and share them.

The maturing leader.—The maturing leader begins to empower others. He does not have the insatiable appetite for recognition and accolades that some have. He learns to share the glory. He turns others loose to do their work without micromanaging details that otherwise would drive him to distraction.

The refocusing leader.—Here the leader evaluates his or her past and future work as a kingdom leader. Acts 28:30-31 (NKJV) states that "Paul dwelt two whole years in his own rented house, and received all who came to him, preaching the kingdom of God and teaching the things which concern the Lord Jesus Christ with all confidence, no one forbidding him." The refocusing leader is prepared for mentoring others.[7]

Mark Corts, pastor of Calvary Baptist Church, Winston-Salem, brings 20–25 ministers together on a regular basis for a design he calls the "Tarheel Ministers Program." It is designed for learning from one another, but Corts has the rare ability to mentor those in the process of learning from one another. He provides the parameters of wisdom, strength, and intelligence that model the learning process. He is forever refocusing his leadership role by sharing his life with others through a mentoring program.

Learning Instruments Can Help

Dozens of instruments are available to help us get in touch with our spiritual gifts.

1. *The Ministry Gifts Inventory System* is available through Convention Press on disk or hard copy. It was first released in 1995. This inventory uses the Bellevue Baptist inventory system as a base. It has been used by ministers and laypersons.

2. Mels Carbonell has a ministry gifts inventory called *Uniquely You.*[8] This inventory has a number of interesting divisions: "Discovering Who You Are," "Interpreting Your Profile," "Biblical Examples/Practical Application," and "Leadership Insights," among others.

3. Richard Byrd has developed the *C and RT Inventory,* or *CREATRIX Inventory,* which defines measurement of leadership gifts and qualities as Challenger, Innovator, Practicalizer, Modifier, Synthesizer, Planner, Reproducer, and Dreamer.[9]

4. Interlink Consultants have developed a Leadership Inventory called *L-E-A-D*, and it is developed around the factors,

> Leader
>
> Expressor
>
> Analyst
>
> Dependable[10]

5. An older instrument that has timeless usefulness was developed by Robert Blake and Jane Mouton, called the *Leadership Grid.*[11] It is built on a nine-point scale of concern for people and concern for production. In the first edition of this book, the application to ministry was made as follows:

> 1-9—Country Club Pastor. Church atmosphere must be friendly.
>
> 1-1—Impoverished Pastor. Minimum effort in relationships and work.
>
> 5-5—Middle of the Road Pastor. Makes comparative analysis and "gets by."

9-1—Task Master Pastor. Lacking in people skills, but "gets things done."

9-9—Equipping Pastor. Gets the most out of the job and helps people accomplish it and get credit for it.[12]

6. The Clergy Program, a Ministry of Palmetto Baptist Medical Center, uses a number of instruments to evaluate leadership gifts and skills, including Meiers-Briggs, Taylor-Johnson, and Minnesota Multiphasic.[13]

7. The Personal and Professional Growth Course at LifeWay Christian Resources has two major leadership inventories training sessions. One is a five-day experience which uses a number of instruments including PF-16, FIRO-B, L-E-A-D, and the Career Assessment Profile (developed by Dr. Fred McGehee, of the North Carolina Baptist Convention). The other experience is a two-day experience using some of the same instruments but in an abbreviated course designed for individuals or couples. The latter is called a Career Assessment.[14]

8. All six Southern Baptist seminaries have placement divisions which assist in evaluating leadership gifts.

9. Most colleges and universities have placement responsibilities which either evaluate or refer for evaluation for leadership gifts and skills.

10. There are dozens of others who will help in leadership evaluation. Contact your state church minister relations director or state executive director for assistance.

Here is a simple leadership analysis to measure skills:

Leadership Skill	Scale for Improvement	Date of Growth
1. Personal Relations	1 2 3 4 5 6 7 8 9 10	_____
2. Listening Skills	1 2 3 4 5 6 7 8 9 10	_____
3. Speaking Skills	1 2 3 4 5 6 7 8 9 10	_____
4. Scheduling Skills	1 2 3 4 5 6 7 8 9 10	_____
5. Empowering Skills	1 2 3 4 5 6 7 8 9 10	_____
6. Celebration Skills	1 2 3 4 5 6 7 8 9 10	_____

7. Learning Skills	1 2 3 4 5 6 7 8 9 10	_____
8. Devotional Skills	1 2 3 4 5 6 7 8 9 10	_____
9. Bible Study Skills	1 2 3 4 5 6 7 8 9 10	_____
10. Family Fun Skills	1 2 3 4 5 6 7 8 9 10	_____
11. Personal Improvement Skills	1 2 3 4 5 6 7 8 9 10	_____
12. Recreation Skills	1 2 3 4 5 6 7 8 9 10	_____
13. Personal Health Skills	1 2 3 4 5 6 7 8 9 10	_____

A Strategy for Improving the Gifts from God

"Only let us live up to what we have already attained" (Phil. 3:16).

The saddest words I ever heard were, "I am disappointed in you." The happiest words I ever heard were, "I am proud of you." Living up to what we have been given from God is an ultimate goal.

Paul talked about improving the gifts from God when he wrote to the church at Colosse, "So then, just as you received Christ Jesus as Lord, continue to live in him, rooted and built up in him, strengthened in the faith as you were taught, and over-flowing with thankfulness" (Col. 2:6). But how? Inquiring ministers want to know. Let us consider the following strategy.

Remember what God has already given you.—He has given you friends, family, optimism, hope, direction, and purpose. He has called you into ministry. He has planned something better than you ever imagined. We must be constantly reminded of this fact. Paul suggested that God will give you what you need. "Therefore you do not lack any spiritual gift" (1 Cor. 1:7). That simple fact is so easy to forget.

Keep up the routines and patterns you have established in your life.—In *Safe Places,* Arterburn, Minirth, and Meier suggest the following:

- Maintain a regular eating schedule.
- Maintain your sleep patterns.
- Maintain sufficient exercise (even when you don't really want to do so).
- Maintain your participation in normal group activities.
- Maintain your good personal habits and routine.[15]

When physiological impairments and difficulties occur, keep the medication consistent with what has been prescribed by your physician. Depression is no longer a closet illness. If you have been prescribed antidepressants and other medications that help you keep depression in check, then by all means, stay with the schedule. Your family and friends deserve it. So do you. You cannot expect to grow if your physiological disposition is out of sync.

Make a daily date with your Bible.—Of course you need to study for sermons, training, discipleship, study courses, and Bible study; but this date needs to include a part of your personal growth.

I have started a plan to study the Bible to find out areas of discovery for my own life. I do not deliberately have a computer, notepad, or pocket date book handy for composing notes, but I am comfortable using these tools for my own benefit and not for preparation for another conference or activity. Some of the approaches have been as follows,

- When I am struggling with feelings of isolation, I have turned to Psalm 19, "The heavens declare the glory of God" (v. 1), or Psalm 21, "For the king trusts in the LORD; through the unfailing love of the Most High he will not be shaken" (v. 7).
- When I am struggling with feelings of sadness, I have turned to John 14, "Do not let your hearts be troubled. Trust in God" (v. 1).
- When I am struggling with feelings of challenge, I have turned to 1 Timothy 4:15, "Be diligent in these matters;

give yourself wholly to them, so that everyone may see your progress."

- When I am experiencing the joy of my life, I have turned to Hebrews 13:6, "The Lord is my helper; I will not be afraid. What can man do to me?"
- When I am struggling with boredom, I have turned to James 3:13, "Who is wise and understanding among you? Let him show it by his good life, by deeds done in the humility that comes from wisdom."
- When I am looking for profound impact words, I have turned to Proverbs.
- When I am looking for comfort, I have turned to Psalms 22, 24, and 73.

Consult with trusted friends and colleagues about changes you are going through.—This step will help you gain balance and perspective. Trusted friends and colleagues will give you feedback that will get your feet back on the ground. Having someone listen to you is affirming in itself. It helps you say out loud what you have been thinking and then will help you get some answers on your own with the help of a caring person.

Pray without ceasing.—The necessity of prayer has always impacted my spiritual life. The practical aspects of prayer have often been confusing. Jesus had much to say about prayer. He taught us how to pray with the Model Prayer. He told us when to pray, and that is not in the front and center positions to be seen of others. He told us where to pray, and that is in our closets and in the privacy of our own lives. But through the years we have turned it into a kind of spiritual shibboleth.

"But when you pray, do not be like the hypocrites, for they love to pray standing in the synagogues and on the street corners to be seen by men" (Matt. 6:5).

The length of prayer should not be a substitute for the depth of prayer. "And when you pray, do not keep on babbling like pagans, for they think they will be heard because of their many words. Do not be like them, for your Father knows what you need before you ask him" (Matt. 6:7-8).

You cannot grow in Christ without maintaining contact with God. You cannot maintain contact with God without prayer. Prayer is communication with God. Listen to His voice. Seek His face. Work for the closeness of His Holy Spirit. Even though He knows what we need before we ask, He waits for our petition because it is God's way of showing us He loves us. Our petition is our approach to God's throne. How can we not grow if we are seeking the presence and will of God?

We would not trivialize prayer by calling it "hanging out with God" as one speaker did. But it does have some of the same passion as "hanging out with friends." Just being with some persons lifts our spirits. In like manner, just being with others cause us to get down in the ditches of despair. But being around where God has acted is a good way to find the presence of God. St. Francis of Assisi was called the patron saint of nature. Trees, flowers, pastures, streams, rivers, oceans, and crops are but a few of the things that remind us of God's creative genius. Hanging out with the creative aspects of God's work remind us of His presence. Sometimes God can speak to us plainly through His creation. Prayer can be a listening experience as well as a requesting experience. Prayer without ceasing is a necessary part of our Christian growth.

In an unpublished paper by Thomas Rodgerson, he suggested that "healthy ministers are committed to a journey of sanctification or spiritual formation."[16] Sanctification is a "setting apart" to God's work. It is a way of discovering what God wants us to do with what He has given us. Prayer is certainly one of the most apparent means for discovering this expedient resource.

Remember that growth is ambiguous.—I like periods in my life. Unfortunately, most of the time I live with commas. Life is full of ambiguities. Life is unfinished. Schubert's *Unfinished* Symphony may have been "unfinished," but it is still a beautiful piece of music in itself. Life is full of unfinished symphonies. But we can enjoy the melodies as they happen.

The work of ministering to others is never finished. I am confused and frustrated by ministers who have complained, "My work is finished in this church." No. It is not finished. You may feel despair, isolation, and loneliness; but your work is not finished. Ministry is forever.

Results are frequently an enigma. How can we know when we have "accomplished"? We can know when we have seen people accept Christ. We can know when we see a new commitment to Christian service by others. But most of the results of ministry are an enigma. We cannot "see" what has happened.

We keep doing the same things over and over again. We keep preparing sermons; preparing for training teachers; building transformational discipleship strategies; teaching leadership courses, seminars for divorced persons, grieving persons, financially challenged persons. But the next week we have to do it over again. We keep doing the things we do repetitively. Why, we ask, can we not do one thing, and "have it done"? Because we are in an ambiguous vocation. The nature of our work is ambiguous. Spiritual growth is difficult to measure.

Pascal wrote in his *Pensees*, "We sail within a vast sphere, ever drifting in uncertainty, driven from end to end. When we think to attach ourselves to any point . . . it wavers and leaves us."[17] And Daniel Taylor commenting on this passage from Pascal in *The Myth of Certainty* wrote, "While certainty is beyond our reach, meaning—something far more valuable—is not. Meaning derives from a right relationship with God, based not on certainty and conformity, but on risk and commitment."[18]

We face the fact that we live in a world of ambiguity. We have to work with uncertainty. But meaning is far more significant in ministry than certainty.

Meaning is the period we are looking for. Ambiguity and uncertainty are the commas that make meaning more powerful.

Read, collect, and file.—To continue to grow, we must read. We must read what is going on in reputable newsmagazines, newspapers, and current events. A church that subscribes to major newsmagazines for their minister(s) is a church that wants their ministers to stay current and interpret the work of Christ in the context of contemporary society.

Stay current in what is being written in Christian theology, biblical studies, homiletics, religious education, archeology. How? Any academic dean in a seminary or a denominational college or universities will gladly share current curriculum requirements. Teachers are responsible for staying current in major areas of study. They will share what the recent releases are because many of them are asked to review books and/or subscribe to professional journals from seminaries. Most of them carry book reviews. Some of these books which have been reviewed will be valuable to your own library. Establish friendships with many of these professors. Most are eager to help ministers who have experienced the travails of a church. They want to be helpful. Many have mentored pastors and staff who have multiple years of experience.

Catalog and categorize subject areas which are vital to your interests and which can help you grow personally and professionally. Newsletters and magazines to help you grow are plentiful. Some of the accomplished magazines that LifeWay Christian Resources of the Southern Baptist Convention publishes are *Church Administration, Growing Churches, The Deacon, Proclaim, Let's Worship, The Minister's Family, Caregiving, Secretary:FYI, Youth Ministry Update, Church Musician Today, Recreation and Sports Ministry Newsletter,* and *Pursuit. Christian Media Journal* has exceptional helps for the pastor and staff in staying abreast of current resources, books, and recent releases.[19] Other publications include *Leadership, The Christian Ministry,* and *American Journal of Pastoral Counseling,* which carries an expansive book review section to help you to know about new releases in the area of pastoral care.

Most major religious publishers release promotional materials which describe their latest releases. Some of the recent publications (free) are the *1998 Academic Catalog from Broadman & Holman, Church Materials Catalog,* published annually by LifeWay Christian Resources of the Southern Baptist Convention.

Other recent publications which are helpful to pastors and staff who work at personal and professional growth are *Fit to Serve Him Longer and Better: A Physical Fitness and Nutrition Guide for Christians; The Team Builder; Building Blocks for Longer Life and Ministry; Surviving and Thriving in Today's Ministry; Evangelism Through the Sunday School: A Journey of Faith; God's Call: The Cornerstone of Effective Ministry; Toolbox for Busy Pastors; Invitation to Christ; Thine Is the Kingdom; Kingdom Principles Growth Strategies; Kingdom Principles for Church Growth; Ministry Gifts Inventory Software Kit; Ministry Gifts Inventory; Kingdom Leadership; Planning Youth Ministry from Boot Up to Exit;* and *Great Commission Evangelism.*[20]

Search the Internet for current trends in religious life, health, theology, and biblical studies. When you discover the Web sites that will be valuable to your personal growth, insert them in your Bookmarks section and retain for your immediate access.

Read. Read. Read. And you will find new areas of interest to your personal growth. Break the addiction to television programming that consumes too much time, and get back in the habit of reading for the sake of personal growth.

Catalog and categorize your areas of interest and the areas of interest of others with whom you work. Build your own filing system. There are accessible filing systems on your computer, but many others are available at your fingertips or the tip of your tongue, if you will ask.

Be accountable to someone.—Yes, we are first accountable to

God. Next we are accountable to ourselves. Then we are accountable to our families. We are accountable to our church. We are accountable to our friends. And the exasperation begins when we begin to see that we are accountable to just about everyone we relate to. But we must have some kind of growth accountability.

I am accountable to my director at LifeWay Christian Resources. As a pastor, I was and am responsible and accountable to the church but more specifically to that group of persons who work closest to me. The deacons, the personnel committee, and another staff person are but a few of the persons who should hold us accountable.

This accountability should have form and substance. It should not just be spontaneous. It should have predictable periods of reporting and planning. At LifeWay we report during "at-home week" each month. As a pastor, I hold frequent staff meetings to discuss accountability. But one-on-one accountability is vital to a personal-growth relationship to the persons to whom we feel responsible. Paul told Titus, "Remind the people to be subject to rulers and authorities, to be obedient, to be ready to do whatever is good" (Titus 3:1).

Paul Meier's book, *Don't Let Jerks Get the Best of You,* has an interesting accountability test called, "The Minirth-Meier Maturity Test," which can help us measure our own progress in spiritual growth. The measurements include: Relational Maturity, Sexual Maturity, Stewardship Maturity, Emotional Maturity, and Moral Maturity. The last measurement, Spiritual Maturity, is adapted here because of its appropriateness.

In taking the test, rate the following statements from 0–3, with 0 meaning "never," 1 meaning "sometimes," 2 meaning "usually," and 3 meaning "nearly always."

    ____ I sincerely desire to serve God, not manipulate Him.

    ____ I accept personal responsibility for my own spiritual growth.

_____ I admit my imperfections and resist temptations to be phony.

_____ I attend church to worship God, not to be entertained, or to entertain others.

_____ I meditate on biblical principles and how they apply to my life and not how to use them in teaching others only.

_____ I seek spiritual instruction to benefit myself, my family, and others.[21]

The three goals used in accountability by Meier are worth repeating because of their relevance:

• Become more like Jesus.

• Seek first the kingdom of God.

• Live one day at a time.[22]

---

[1] Stephen Arterburn, Frank Minirth, and Paul Meier, _Safe Places_ (Nashville: Thomas Nelson, 1997), 218.

[2] Ibid.

[3] Ibid.

[4] William J. Bennett, _Our Sacred Honor_ (Nashville: Broadman & Holman, 1997), 35.

[5] Neil Knierim, _God's Call: The Cornerstone of Effective Ministry_ (Nashville: Convention, 1998), 21.

[6] Ibid.

[7] Mike Miller, _Kingdom Leadership_ (Nashville: Convention Press, 1996), 80–89.

[8] For more information about Mels Carbonell, _Uniquely You,_ write him at P. O. Box 490, Blue Ridge, GA.

[9] For more information about Richard Byrd, _CREATRIX Inventory,_ write him at 350 Sansome Street, San Francisco, CA 94104-1342.

[10] For more information about _L-E-A-D,_ write Interlink, P. O. Box 23586, Overland Park, KS 66282-2586.

[11] _Leadership Grid_ (Houston: Gulf Publishing, 1964).

[12] Brooks R. Faulkner, _Getting on Top of Your Work_ (Nashville: Convention, 1974), 139–42.

[13] For more information, write The Clergy Program, a Ministry of Palmetto Baptist Medical Center, Taylor at Marion Street, Columbia, SC 29220.

[14] For more information, contact LeaderCare, LifeWay Christian Resources of the Southern Baptist Convention, 127 Ninth Ave., North, Nashville, TN 37234. 615-251-2265.

[15] Arterburn, Minirth, and Meier, 148–50.

[16] Thomas Rodgerson, "Working Paper on Healthy Religion, Churches, and Ministers," October 1998: 5.

[17] Blaise Pascal, _Pensees_ (New York: E. P. Dutton, 1958), 64.

[18] Daniel Taylor, _The Myth of Certainty_ (Grand Rapids: Zondervan, 1992), 94.

[19] For more information or to order any of these periodicals, call 800-458-2772.

[20] For more information or to order any of these resources, call 800-458-2772.

[21] Paul Meier, _Don't Let Jerks Get the Best of You_ (Nashville: Thomas Nelson, 1993), 231.

[22] Ibid., 232–35.

LEAVING WITH GRACE

TIPS

1	"Forgetting what is behind and straining toward what is ahead, I press on" (Phil. 3:13-14).
2	There is security in familiarity, but progress is in unchartered waters.
3	The leap of faith in ministry is searching for what God will do next with your life.
4	Prepare for the future to avoid getting bogged down in the past.
5	Treat leaving like a roller-coaster ride; even when the bottom drops out, it can be thrilling.
6	The family of the minister who is leaving needs much attention.
7	Leaving gives us the luxury of the absence of suffering over mistakes.
8	If a cat can land on its feet after a six-foot drop, even more will a minister who has been blessed of God.
9	You have a choice. Remember broken promises, or build hope for the future.
10	Vindictiveness is a poor substitute for forgiveness.
11	When you start new, start with a clean slate.
12	Hang out with friends if the transition is difficult.
13	Leaving isn't so bad; it's starting over that's hard.
14	You may leave a church; God will never leave you.

Anyone can begin a ministry at a church with grace. The real test is, Can you leave a church with grace?

For 20 years we have been studying forced termination seriously and deliberately. Some patterns have emerged that can teach us about leaving with grace.

The most prevalent reason for a minister's leaving a church, described by both ministers and laypersons, is a struggle for leadership. It is a control issue: Who is going to run the church?

The five most common causes of forced termination (which have not changed significantly since the first research projects conducted by the Sunday School Board in 1981) are:

1. Control issues—Who's going to run the church?
2. Poor people skills on the part of the pastor.
3. Church's resistance to change.
4. Pastor's leadership style—too strong.
5. Church was already conflicted when the pastor arrived.[1]

By its nature, forced termination lays the groundwork for a hostile takeover and then an adversarial transition for the minister and family. It is difficult—nearly impossible—to leave with grace. But it is possible with the right ingredients.

"Forgetting what is behind and straining toward what is ahead, I press on" (Phil. 3:13-14). Paul left harsh critics. But he also left people who loved him. It is as hard to leave the critics as it is to leave those who love us. Why? Because as caring persons, we do not like to leave things unsettled. We want to leave in a good humor. It is hard to leave knowing that we could have solved the spiritual problems of persons' lives. We miss the people who love us. We long for their presence. We also miss not having settled issues which have disrupted our ministry.

How do we leave with grace? We leave our mothers' wombs to breathe the breath of life. We leave our incubated homes to start the learning process in preschool. We leave home to complete the educational process in college. We leave home permanently (in most cases) when we begin a family. We leave the formal educational process to begin a vocation. We often leave one vocation to enter another. Leaving is an intrusion on our lives, an invasion of our privacy. Leaving with grace is difficult, but it is possible.

"Do not boast about tomorrow, for you do not know what a

day may bring forth" (Prov. 27:1). The writer must have had ministers in mind. You just never know what tomorrow will bring.

Here are some practical suggestions for leaving with grace.

Don't Overstay Your Welcome

"Seldom set foot in your neighbor's house—too much of you, and he will hate you" (Prov. 25:17). That is another way of saying: "Don't overstay your welcome. Don't invade others' privacy." Like a sitcom on television that viewers quickly tire of, the minister can become too much with the members unless careful.

God is never finished with us. He always has something better planned. However, the chemistry between a minister and a church is sometimes so volatile that it can erupt unless monitored closely and carefully. There is a bottom line. Sometimes it is best for everyone if the minister leaves a church. It may be painful. Children may have to leave friends and school. Spouses may have to leave jobs. But some minister-church marriages do not work. Leaving is simply best for all concerned.

Jesus said it clearly: "And if any place will not welcome you or listen to you, shake the dust off your feet when you leave, as a testimony against them" (Mark 6:11).

Some mixes just simply do not work. These mixes can become toxic. They are poisonous to the work of the ministry. They are poisonous to the growth of the church. They are poisonous to relationships. It does not happen often, but it does happen.

If conversations continue to harass your comfort zone as you try to sleep, you may want to consider the possibility that your relationship with your church is toxic. If you can decipher the difference between normal periods of paranoia and periods of spiritual stalking of your peace by those who "know what is best for your church," and the latter prevails, you need to consider the possibility that your relationship with your church is toxic. The bottom line is, If your church is making you miserable, you may need to consider one of two possibilities—therapy or departure.

If Possible, Work Out Your Differences

The Bible has a plan. Matthew 18:15-17 suggests that you go to the person with whom you have an issue. If that does not work, take someone with you. If that does not work, let the church deal with the issue.

You and the church should decide if a conflict mediator would be helpful. If the situation can be salvaged, a conflict mediator can offer guidance. Contact your church minister relations director in the state convention or LeaderCare at LifeWay Christian Resources for a third-person conflict mediator. It is a process that has worked for many churches.[2] If at all possible, work it out.

Do not resign impulsively. Your family, your church, and you will suffer. Ministers are sensitive. If they are hurt, they tend to recoil into a spiritual fetal position and play martyr. That is not a strategy. That is a cop-out. Do not resign impulsively.

Jim had been doing most things right. He had positive results. More than 30 persons had accepted Christ during a three-month period. Forty-two other persons had moved their membership. Attendance had grown from 180 in worship to more than 300. People were witnessing. Bible study was focused. Discipleship was again important. But then the bottom fell out.

Two long-term deacons asked for a private appointment. They came to him as "spokespersons" for the church. "We feel it is time for you to go," said the first. This deacon had been in the church for more than 45 years and was respected by many.

The second added: "People are not happy with the contemporary worship. You are the first minister we have ever had who did not wear a tie on Sunday night. We don't like singing from a PowerPoint presentation. What's wrong with the hymnal?"

Jim was crushed. He went home to his wife and wept. He called two of his closest allies in the church. Both were amazed that these two men were "spokespersons" for the church. They said. "They do not represent the attitude of the whole church."

"Yes," they added, "A few are unhappy." But the idea of reaching people for Christ was celebrated among most members.

"If they don't want me, I will go," he said. They reasoned with him. When change is dramatic, people need time to adjust.

That Sunday night he was prepared to resign. These men had been in the church for decades. Their children were there. It did not matter that one of Jim's allies was the son of one of the deacons. He prepared his resignation. He used the language of Zion in his preparation. "I believe God is leading me to leave. No, I do not have a place to go yet, but God will find a place for me."

Fortunately, one of the allies persuaded his dad to recant. The father and son came to Jim and asked him to reconsider. Some soul-searching, praying, and crying followed. Some issues were settled. The contemporary worship was toned down but not dramatically. Jim wore a tie on alternate Sunday nights. Concessions were made on both sides. Jim stayed. The church continues to grow—not without problems, but the church continues to grow.

In this case it was possible for a pastor to work out the differences between himself and some of the members. Not all cases turn out this well. Many pastors try to resolve problems but end up with broken hearts and resign. Some of those resignations are probably premature. God has always been able to work through our mistakes and our immature decisions to use the people He has called to accomplish His will and purpose. The kingdom of God is bigger than our neurotic humanity. Thank goodness.

Include Others in the Decision-Making Process

"Two are better than one, because they have a good return for their work: If one falls down, his friend can help him up. But pity the man who falls and has no one to help him up! . . . Though one may be overpowered, two can defend themselves. A cord of three strands is not quickly broken" (Eccl. 4:9-10, 12).

Get the advice of legitimizers in the church. If those you respect feel the case is terminal, then seek out a solution for leaving that is most redemptive and restorative for all. Do not leave out the people you have trusted in other decision-making issues in the church. They deserve to be a part of this historical event.

"I thought we were friends," a young deacon told the pastor after he had announced his resignation. "How could you do this without talking with me first?"

The pastor said it had not occurred to him that the deacon would feel slighted. They had been through some rough waters together, and the young deacon felt that he should have been considered in the decision to resign. He was probably right.

Once while I was working with a minister of education and his wife, she confided to me that he had not even consulted her before announcing his resignation. That is inexcusable. Trust others to give advice when you are considering leaving. They deserve to be in on the decision. This is true especially for one's family.

Prepare for the Future

Getting bogged down in the past is easy. Prepare for the future. Stonewall issues that have negative bearing on your attitude. Work on your attitude first, so that you can prepare for the future.

Remember, there is nothing new under the sun except the history you missed. It is okay to remember the past, just don't get bogged down in it so that it becomes an obsession. Remember, "Those who hope in the LORD will renew their strength. They will soar on wings like eagles; they will run and not grow weary, they will walk and not be faint" (Isa. 40:31).

When Abraham was at his wits' end, he remained obedient to God, but all looked futile. His only son was about to be sacrificed. Abraham told his son that God would provide. Sure enough, He did. God provided a ram caught in a thicket. Later Abraham called the place Jahweh Jireh, "'The LORD Will Provide.' And to this day it is said, 'On the mountain of the LORD it will be provided'" (Gen. 22:14). When things look the bleakest, God will always come through. He will provide. Therefore, do your best to get prepared for the future, and trust God to provide the details.

Call your friends. Call church minister relations directors, or executive directors of state conventions if your state does not have a church minister relations director. Call the seminary you attended. Call directors of missions. Tell them your story. Ask them to pray for you. Ask them to tell your story to others. Begin planning for the future. Think about some of the options available to you.

This would be a good time to do a career assessment. The cost is minimal and in many cases can be subsidized by your state convention. The assessment takes two days The purpose is to discover the gifts and skills that will help you survive in another vocation until you can find a place to serve.[3]

Get Ready for the Grief Experience

In a sense, you have experienced a death. The vocational relationship to your church has died. Relationships that were meaningful no longer exist. Your spouse and children will suffer grief experiences. All of your family should get ready for the grief experience.

Denial.—One of the first stages of grief is denial: "This is what God wants." "This is best for all of us." "We will know in the future how God has worked this out." Romans 8:28 will now become real.

Of course, all of these statements are true. But we have been programmed because of our vocation to say these things. It isn't that we do not believe them. We do. It is simply that we are programmed to say the things we think we ought to say, while at the same time we deny the reality of the pain. How can we make house payments? How will we feed out family? How will we pay for the kids' lunches? insurance? taxes? It goes on—until finally, we begin to get a more realistic picture.

Only then are we ready for the next step.

Anger.—Unfulfilled dreams in the church, closure to relationships, and feelings of being mistreated are some of the more prominent reasons for anger. Sometimes the anger is pushed down so deeply that it causes other symptoms, like overeating, high blood pressure, insomnia, and frequent headaches, to name a few.

Someone has to be the heavy, the target of the anger. If not careful, family members begin to take the anger out on one another. It is better to have an inanimate object or a ghost of a culprit. In other words, be angry at someone or something you will not be seeing until you can work through a healthy dose of anger. You will not want to retaliate even though that possibility will be tempting. Retaliation is like a poisonous snake. It will come back and bite you when you least expect it.

"In your anger do not sin. Do not let the sun go down while you are still angry" (Eph. 4:26). The meaning is, don't "incubate" anger. If you store it, it will become *miseo* or hate, resentment, even rage. Find some outlets to relieve the pressure of the anger. Walk, jog, play, find new hobbies. Find the things that will elevate fun in your life and dissipate the negative feelings.

Although it is a myth that time heals all hurts, it does have a way of putting things in perspective. Distance between you and the church is imperative. To remain as a church member after termination is masochistic. It invites pain and humiliation. Get out of town and away from the painful visual memories.

Depression.—Turning the anger inward is normal. When that happens, depression results. Depression is the acceptance of blame and fault. "I deserve this" can become a recurring nightmare in all relationships.

Depression can take many forms. The more common form of depression present with termination is "episodic," and fortunately, it does not last. If it becomes more severe, by all means see a physician, preferably a therapist.

Acceptance of some responsibility in the trauma of grief is healthy and realistic. Acceptance of all the responsibility is too heavy a burden to bear. Depression has a way of loading up all the baggage of guilt and carrying it alone. No one deserves all the blame for a the ending of a relationship with a church. Spread it out. Handle it biblically. Do the right thing. Then move on.

Bargaining.—"Lord, if you will just find me another church quickly, I will. . ." "This would be a good time to have an offer of temporary employment. If only. . ."

Bargaining takes place at several intervals. Much of the bargaining has probably already been going on. I will change my relationship to these persons, and perhaps it will save my ministry. If I say these things, then things will be different.

Concessions.—Few grief experts concede that there is a step after bargaining. This step may be called "concessions." After bargaining begins to feel strained, the grief experience includes some concessions. For example, it becomes apparent that playing the lottery is not an option. Not only is it contrary to your ethical and moral values, it is a fantasy and not a reality.

Then it becomes clear that a larger opportunity is not just around the corner waiting for your decision. The bargaining begins to hit several stone walls.

A sardonic but amusing quip, often attributed to Mark Twain, is "Friends come and go; enemies accumulate." It is too cynical to be placed in this grief context, but one of the bargaining dead ends is, "Enemies finally become friends." Don't count on it.

When Paul wrote, "Be kind and compassionate to one another, forgiving each other, just as in Christ God forgave you" (Eph. 4:32), it did not mean that everything would be washed clean and the job status would be back as it was. Some enemies enjoy the prolonged ride. There must be "concessions," a reality check.

Elihu, the fourth of Job's adversaries, spoke to the folly of bargaining. "Men cry out under a load of oppression; they plead for relief from the arm of the powerful. But no one says, Where is God my Maker, who gives songs in the night?" (Job 35:9). The meaning is, If you don't praise God before you are in trouble, you are already in trouble. Don't waste your breath searching for help if you have not paid the price of praise when things are tough. Bargaining is folly if you have not laid the foundation of holding God in praise and adoration. Elihu assumed that Job had failed and was giving him a lesson in the absolute futility of bargaining.

In most cases, bargaining is the cry of a desperate person. Concessions become the alternative. Elihu continued, "The godless in heart harbor resentment; . . . but those who suffer he delivers in their suffering; he speaks to them in their affliction" (Job. 36:13, 15). Grief may be the time when you are closest to God. Do not try to dispense with it prematurely. It may be your open door to God. Rejoice in your affliction. God will not forsake you or leave you. Your adversity could be the blessing disguised in deception.

Resolution.—It is painful. Moving to the home of parents for a period of time is humiliating. The admission that in this situation, in this particular church, it "did not work out" is, indeed, painful. It is sometimes devastating. One pastor's son, 18, left in the middle of his senior year. When I talked with him, he scared me with the statement, "I just don't think life is worth living." It was the cry of a desperate person. If he was feeling this way, then the pastor and wife must have been harboring similar feelings.

That situation had a happy ending. He got help through one of our LeaderCare network counselors. The young man, his parents, and a sister got involved in some resolution activities. They moved across town, and he enrolled in another school. He has now finished his senior year in high school in a comfortable environment, but making new friends was difficult.

Resolution is facing the toughest alternatives and making the best of the situation. The Lord said to Job in the midst of these horrible conversations, "Who is this that darkens my counsel with words without knowledge? . . . Where were you when I laid the earth's foundation? Tell me, if you understand" (Job. 38:2, 4). The meaning is: "Don't you know that I have a bigger plan than you could imagine? I was here before knowledge began. I know what I am doing. Have faith. Trust Me. I will bring you through."

These are comforting words when you have lost your home, and your wife has lost her friends, and your children have pulled up their roots from school and transferred to another. The salary may have halted temporarily, but God's love is enduring. You may have to borrow money, but God will bring you through. Have faith. Trust Him. He will endure. So will you.

I was talking with one minister of music who had been terminated. "Brooks," he said. "You have no idea how hard it is when you are concerned about how you are going to come up with lunch money for your daughter who is the president of the sophomore class in her high school. You don't want her to be humiliated, but if you don't have it, you don't have it."

That will grip your heart. It did mine. Sometimes I would give a limb if I could fix some situations.

Tap Available Resources for Temporary Survival

Directors of missions are your friends. Work with them. Church minister relations directors in state conventions can be indispensable. They have contacts with churches who are willing to help. Several organizations provide temporary help. Antioch Affection is one. This plan has helped terminated ministers and families serve in a ministry position while getting back on their feet. State conventions provide emergency funds for rent and food.

Wounded Heroes, started by Freddie Gage in Texas, has provided psychiatric evaluation and encouragement to pastors, other ministers, and spouses, while getting them back on their feet emotionally, but especially spiritually.

Don't neglect the power of the Scriptures. You have encouraged others with Psalms, Proverbs, Romans 8, Matthew 5–7, 1 John 1, Ephesians, 2 Corinthians 4, and now it is time to be encouraged by them. Let them simmer in your consciousness.

Find a good devotional book to read daily until you get your perspective back. Calvin Miller has written one entitled *Until He Comes*. It will encourage you during this transition. One of the devotionals is entitled, "Today Is the Only Place We May Live." The passage is Matthew 6:34. The prayer he relates is, "Lord Jesus, I have wasted so much of my life worrying about problems that never came. I have counted too much on the mine I thought I would discover; I never saw the gold about my feet. I want today to be defined in grace, so that tomorrow has its proper place."[4]

Take Care of Your Body During This Time

When you are leaving a special place or special work, you will be tempted to neglect the important things. Your body is one of those. Take care of your body.

Recently, I ran across a marvelous statement: "If you don't take care of your body, where else are you going to live?" That is a great lesson for ministers. The potential of becoming overweight by eating your troubles away will be ever present. Obesity is the bane of many ministers. Most of us do not smoke or drink alcoholic beverages, but we do damage to our bodies by overeating. During times of crisis, it is even more prevalent.

Eat right. Eat breakfast. Avoid eating between meals. Get a nutritionist to work with you during the transition.

It is enough to remember, "Do you not know that your body is a temple of the Holy Spirit, who is in you, whom you have received from God? You are not your own; you were bought at a price. Therefore honor God with your body" (1 Cor. 6:19-20).

Negotiate a Financial Package

If conflict is serious, you will be tempted to neglect this aspect. But you can still leave with grace and have your family and your own personal needs taken care of if you handle it with diplomacy.

Many churches have been encouraged by termination and transition advice to develop a termination package. Some are generous. One year's salary is the longest package I have seen. Several provide six months' severance pay. But a three-month severance package is the least of a church's obligations.

You probably are not in a position to bargain for this severance package. But your allies will be. This will be an opportunity for some in the church to allow the church to have some dignity in the termination. It will also allow you to have your own personal needs taken care of in the transition. Work with persons whom you trust to work for you. Be open and candid with your needs. Show them a bank statement to allow them access to your personal needs. Of course, you will want to ask them to be protective of this information. But allowing them to see your personal needs will give them an opportunity to affirm you and your family.

Many directors of missions can play a vital role in this transition. Trusted directors of missions can supplement the information needed for a church to be generous.

Don't Look Back

There is a time to say hello and a time to say goodbye. Whether you leave under strained circumstances or under positive circumstances, saying goodbye is vital for the new minister.

As a pastor, I have made some mistakes. I have gone back for funerals and weddings. I have regretted some of these events. It is possible to work out a diplomatic situation. Having two ministers in a wedding or funeral is not unusual. The new pastor will not mind if the families are special friends to the church members.

One of those areas we least like to examine is the loss of power and esteem. Some ministers are so identified with what they do that separating who they are from what they do is nearly impossible. Transitions offer an opportunity to examine our own faith and the strength of our spirit. Temporarily, if we have been forced to terminate, we will have lost our role as leader and shepherd.

Even in a smooth transition, when going from one church to another after resignation, those who trusted us look at us with new eyes and ears. They are suspicious. They feel rejected. They feel betrayed, even in the best of circumstances. Consequently, the esteem with which they held us is either suspect or gone. We need to be emotionally and spiritually braced for this possibility.

At this time, maintain some sense of consistency. Even when others are hostile, avoid being defensive. Even when they are passive or withdrawn, make an effort to be the same person you have been. That is grace. That is leaving with grace. Grace is the ability to see things as they could be and to believe that God's fingerprints have been on the worst things to bring about His purpose. What looks bad to us may be meant for good in God's plan.

---

[1] The 1998 research was conducted by LeaderCare in cooperation with state convention church minister relations directors and associational directors of missions. Cliff Tharp, LifeWay Christian Resources, directed the research with Norris Smith of LeaderCare.

[2] For more information, contact LeaderCare, LifeWay Christian Resources of the Southern Baptist Convention, 127 Ninth Ave., North, Nashville, TN 37234. Phone: 615-251-2265.

[3] For more information about Career Assessment, contact LeaderCare.

[4] Calvin Miller, *Until He Comes* (Nashville: Broadman & Holman, 1998), day 81.

CELEBRATING VICTORIES

TIPS

1	Accomplishments should be earmarked by celebration.
2	Celebration is best when everybody wins.
3	Celebration is most apparent when the spirit of generosity is evident.
4	Hidden agendas deflate celebration.
5	When celebrating anniversaries of church staff, be sure to give proper attention to personal achievements.
6	Trust ensures the intensity of celebration.
7	Unexpected celebrations are more memorable.
8	Maintenance and restoration of faith should never be underestimated in causes for celebration.
9	It's OK, but not absolutely essential, to have fun when you celebrate.
10	Celebration is an expression of kindness.
11	Overcoming adversity is cause for celebration.
12	Unselfishness is the most representative symptom of celebration.
13	Don't refuse to be a recipient of celebration; it gives others an opportunity to express kindness.

Why do Baptists feel guilty when they celebrate? Of course, not all do. But many do.

The Old Testament is full of celebration. "I lift up my eyes to the hills—where does my help come from? My help comes from the LORD, the Maker of heaven and earth" (Ps. 121:1).

That is celebration.

"God is the strength of my heart and my portion forever" (Ps. 73:26).

That is celebration.

Hannah celebrated when she dedicated Samuel. "So now I give him to the LORD. For his whole life he will be given over to the LORD" (1 Sam. 1:28).

Many churches have celebrated by participating in activities which to some may seem strange, perhaps even bizarre: old-fashioned services, roof-top experiences, growing beards. I even heard of one church that asked their pastor to wrestle a pig (the animal, not to be confused with other living beings), and he did. These events came as the result of high attendance day, reaching a financial or mission goal, or burning a note on a loan.

There are many ways to celebrate. Some are better than others. It is sad to see a church that does not know how to celebrate.

A Definition of Celebration

A celebration should earmark an activity as a joyous event. Perhaps the best biblical definition is this: "These were all commended for their faith, yet none of them received what had been promised. God had planned something better for us so that only together with us would they be made perfect" (Heb. 11:39-40). A celebration is an event that is a commendation for being faithful because God has something better planned. It is hope.

Webster defines *celebration* as "To demonstrate satisfaction by festivities or other deviation from routine." "Festivities" suggests it should be fun. A celebration should earmark an event by some form of festivity or fun.

The New York Yankees baseball team won more games than any baseball team in history in 1998. The ticker-tape parade and festivities that followed were the beginning of a long celebration. Mark MaGuire and Sammy Sosa hit 70 and 66 home runs respectively in 1998; the drama on television was breathtaking. No Hollywood movie plot could have captured the event when MaGuire broke Roger Maris' record and went directly into the stands to "celebrate" with the family of Roger Maris. Then, to cap it off, the person who was competing with MaGuire, Sosa, came in from right field to congratulate MaGuire. What a "happening."

We have celebrations in churches too. When someone is won to Christ, we celebrate. This is especially true for those we have sought after, prayed for, and coaxed into coming to Christ. We sense a victory in Jesus Christ. It should be cause for celebration. Conjuring up excitement should not be necessary. The anticipation that leads to the victory should cause the celebration to accelerate. It is cause for celebration for the cloud of witnesses, and it should be cause for celebration for those who are still here.

Therefore, a good definition of *celebration* is "the fun you have in remembering accomplishments, events, or personal achievements which are done in an atmosphere with festive and congratulatory happenings." Here is a more applicable definition: "Blessed is the man who perseveres under trial, because when he has stood the test, he will receive the crown of life that God has promised to those who love him" (Jas. 1:12).

As Baptists, or for that matter, as Christians in general, we need a lot of help in learning to celebrate.

To Celebrate, Develop the Right Attitude

"We had 250 in Bible study last Sunday. That is the most we have had in 11 years. I'm thinking about shaving my head if I can get the deacons to follow suit." He may have been only half serious, but he was enjoying the moment. He was having fun. He was caught up in the celebration.

The pastors who were listening at the Monday morning pastor's conference were enjoying the moment as well.

Then it happened. "That's nothing. We had 349 yesterday. What do you think of that?" As I reflected on the atmosphere of the crowd, I think most of the pastors there were embarrassed for the enthusiastic pastor who had 349. Why?

One of the reasons celebration is so difficult is that we have to give others the limelight. We have to permit others to be front and center. That is especially difficult for pastors and staff because our vocational handicap is that we are thrust in front of crowds and congregations. The pastor with 349 tried to steal the thunder. The other pastors saw this insipid attempt to celebrate as braggadocio and blustery. More than that, it was insensitive to the pastor who was applauding the accomplishments of his church.

Rudyard Kipling said that both triumph and defeat are impostors.[1] We can add something to that. Either triumph or defeat can be earmarked as a step of personal growth in the Christian pilgrimage. The problem in celebration is one of attitude in either triumph or defeat. If triumph must be at the expense of another (as in the case of the 349 over the 250), then it is an "imposter." We would all wish for the second pastor to be able to rejoice in the accomplishments of the first without comparison. In comparing we develop an attitude that devastates celebration. "God opposes the proud but gives grace to the humble" (Jas. 4:6). Only the humble can truly celebrate. The attitude of celebration must be one of humility. It must not compare. It must rejoice in the events and accomplishments of others.

The anticipation of God's purposive direction in His kingdom gives us the freedom to celebrate with others. The movie *Chariots of Fire* tells the story of Eric Liddell. Refusing to run the 100-meter race in the 1924 Olympics on Sunday because of his religious convictions, he entered the 400-meter on Monday and won the gold medal by 5 meters, setting a new world record and bringing home England's first gold medal. They called him "The Flying Scotsman." The movie itself was a celebration.

At 43 years of age, Liddell died in Weihsien Concentration Camp because of his associations with missionaries in China. Who can forget the award-winning music that accompanied that great story of celebration? Who can forget the story of Eric Liddell, who gave life and conviction a whole new lift?

The purposive direction of God's kingdom makes stories like Eric Liddell's celebrative. It is the attitude of anticipation and unselfishness. It is humility. It is loving others as we love ourselves.

Generosity Is the Best Foundation for Celebration

Who said, "The only thing worth keeping is what you give away"? Why is the generous person so admired? On the other hand, why is generosity so difficult to capture as a Christian trait?

But generosity must have limits. Going broke doesn't express generosity. Therefore, it is not celebration. Going broke brings on an entirely different set of difficulties. Celebration comes from receiving the benefits of generosity which can be given without depriving the giver of life sustenance.

Paul wrote to Timothy about the celebration of generosity: "Command those who are rich in this present world not to be arrogant nor to put their hope in wealth, which is so uncertain, but to put their hope in God, who richly provides us with everything for our enjoyment. Command them to do good, to be rich in good deeds, and to be *generous* and willing to share" (1 Tim. 6:17-18, italics mine). Then Paul promised the celebration: "In this way they will lay up treasure for themselves as a firm foundation for the coming age, so that they may take hold of the life that is truly life" (v. 19).

Being generous has its own reward. It is more blessed to give than to receive. My wife and granddaughter joined me in an afternoon of scavenger hunting. We were in the Beanie Baby craze, and Brooke was vitally interested in capturing the Princess Di Beanie Baby. Almost a dozen flea-market stops proved fruitless. We were about to go home empty handed. The last flea-market attendant told us where some Beanie Babies had been available earlier that morning. Fatigue was a factor, but we decided it would be worth the 25-minute drive.

The first booth had some, but no Princess Di. The attendant said, "Another booth has some." She had a strange look on her face that said, "But you wouldn't want to go there." When I questioned her, she said the Princess Di Beanie Baby is expensive.

There was only one Princess Di, and it was far too expensive. As Brooke and I walked away, I could see the disappointment on her face. Her grandmother had already given up and was shopping for other less expensive items. The attendant had already shown us the "no negotiation" sign on the cost of the Princess Di.

I reasoned that we had spent almost an entire day on the search. We had planned on spending at least $50 because it was uncirculated. We were not prepared for the $105 price tag. After watching Brooke's face for several minutes, I went back. I told the lady we were not prepared to pay $105, but I would give her $65.

"I'm sorry," she said, "But I would make no profit." I understood that reasoning and was about to walk away.

"Would you give $85?"

"No," I said. Then both of us, both the woman and I, looked at Brooke at the same time. A little bitty tear was the only response she had. Then Brooke said, "It's okay, PawPaw, we tried."

"Okay," the woman said. "$65."

Then I heard myself say, "That's OK; let's make it $75."

Everybody was happy. We found her grandmother. We celebrated. I felt good. Brooke felt good. Her grandmother felt good. And, I think, the woman who sold us Princess Di felt good. Generosity, even when it is your own, sets the stage for celebration.

Get Rid of the Garbage Before Celebration

A father and his six-year-old son were passing by a garbage dump. Automobiles were lined up for two blocks.

"What is this place?" asked Zach.

"This is a garbage drop for people who can't afford garbage pick up, " said the father.

"Wow! This is a happening place," said Zach.

As the father was telling the story, he suggested it would be therapeutic to take all our emotional and spiritual garbage to a drop instead of waiting for the church to pick it up and haul it off.

There are many forms and kinds of garbage—envy and jealousy, conflict and anger, resentment and bitterness. Look at the list of garbage in Galatians 5: "The acts of the sinful nature are obvious: sexual immorality, impurity and debauchery; idolatry and witchcraft; hatred, discord, jealousy, fits of rage, selfish ambition, dissensions, factions and envy; drunkenness, orgies, and the like." Then Paul warned, "I warn you, as I did before, that those who live like this will not inherit the kingdom of God" (vv. 19-21).

You simply cannot join in the celebration of life until you dump this garbage. But then, the good news—the celebration: "But the fruit of the Spirit is love, joy, peace, patience, kindness, goodness, faithfulness, gentleness and self-control" (Gal. 5:22-23).

Anything which draws our attention away from godliness and the works of the Spirit will eventually develop into garbage. Real celebration without dumping this garbage is impossible. An office party at Christmas time that entices others to act immorally or with no inhibitions is not celebration. Genuine Christian celebration is that which affords the grace of God to activate our repentance so that we get rid of the garbage of life's distractions.

One dangerous result of collecting garbage without dumping it is depression. It creeps up on the minister who deals with church members' difficult personal issues. Charles Figley, a therapist who works extensively with the FBI, wrote *Compassion Fatigue.* Some of the hard-to-recognize symptoms of depression he suggests are "fatigue and physical depletion/exhaustion, sleep difficulties, specific somatic problems such as headaches, gastrointestinal disturbances, colds, and flu." Additionally, "emotional symptoms include irritability, anxiety, depression, guilt, and a sense of helplessness." Behavioral symptoms are "aggression, callousness, pessimism, defensiveness, cynicism, and substance abuse." Work-related symptoms include "quitting the job [or being terminated as in the case of many ministers, or for that matter, resigning without a place to go], poor work performance, absenteeism, tardiness, misuse of work breaks, and thefts."[2]

What can be done about this undumped garbage? A therapist is certainly an option. The stigma of getting professional help for a minister is no longer insurmountable. If the symptoms are serious enough, then by all means, get professional help. Your church will love you for it in the long run.

Figley offered some practical guidelines. First he called it "vicarious traumatization."[3] This means "getting in bed with the patient" or taking on the symptoms of hurt and pain of the church members we try to help. He suggested:

"Develop personal strategies to develop safety, trust, esteem, intimacy, and control."[4]—Do this before you expend all your energy on compassion. If you do not, you will expend all your energy prematurely and have nothing left to give.

"Maintain a personal life."[5]—You are not married to the church. That is your work and your calling. You are married to your spouse, and you are responsible for your family. Give them first priority. Their needs come first. Then you will be free to minister to your church. You cannot be divided by indecision about which needs are paramount. Your family is first. Enough said.

"Use personal psychotherapy."[6]—Group therapy and support groups have been indispensable to my work with pastors, families, and staff. I have also needed personal psychotherapy. Periodically and regularly, I have sought and received psychotherapy for my own needs. People who work with dispensing compassion must have a place to dump their own needs to free them up to deal with the needs of others. You deserve care. You deserve the taste of

God's grace. Seeking help is not demeaning. It is a way of dumping your own garbage for the express purpose of freeing yourself and others for the glorious event of celebration.

"Identify healing activities." [7]—To name a few: art; music; time with friends, family, and especially children; keeping a journal; enjoying nature; traveling; taking time off; hobbies; going to movies; watching television without feeling guilty; golf; tennis; recreational activities, such as hiking, swimming, surfing, mountain climbing; exercising; dancing (unless culturally taboo); and a massage. There are many more. My wife loves to craft. That is a verb. She doesn't really look for an item. She looks, period. That is crafting. Occasionally, she finds "something" she really likes, and if she can afford it, she buys it. This is her "healing activity."

Prayer is a remarkably healing activity, but I fear that many lose the healing aspects in their personal, conceptual trauma of pharisaism. The motivation seems to be more to pray in order to tell others, rather than to pray for the healing it does for us.

"Tend to your spiritual needs." [8]—And this is really big. "The spiritual damage, or the loss of meaning, connection, and hope, that can signal vicarious traumatization is profoundly destructive, and attending to one's spiritual health is critical to survival and growth." He added, "Find. . . a way to restore faith in something larger than oneself, whether by reconnecting with the best of all that is human, with nature, or with spiritual entity." [9] In our case, we reconnect with God. God has definitely not disconnected with us, but occasionally we lose touch with the closeness of the grace of God. When we do, we have compassion fatigue.

Celebration Is a "Disconnect Activity"

Tommy Yessick, in his dissertation, developed the idea of "The Relationship Between Leisure Disposition and Total Well-Being in Middle-Aged Adults." He suggested that a disconnect activity is essential to celebration. Leisure, he said, has no purpose "except to disconnect." When we disconnect, we renew our strength. That is when God is most operative. We are in a listening mode. We know God wants to get through to us, but we expend too much energy trying to get through to Him. When we have disconnect activity, we free ourselves so that God can get through to us.

Yessick suggested five characteristics of a leisure disposition.

"Perceived competence."—We know we can golf. Perhaps not well. But we can swing the club.

"Perceived control."—We can get on the course. We know most of the rules. We are able to manipulate the events. We are in charge of our own destiny.

"We know our leisure needs."—We get some gratification from playing, even if we play poorly. We know we need to disconnect for the express purpose of restoring some objectivity.

"Depth of involvement."—We get so engrossed in the activity that we forget we have two angry deacons who do not like the way we have suggested the change in the worship activity.

"Sense of playfulness."—We are letting our "child" out to play for no specific purpose.[10]

"The fruit of the Spirit is love, joy, peace, patience, kindness, goodness, faithfulness, gentleness and self-control" (Gal. 5:22).

Celebration Is Playfulness

Yessick developed four domains of playfulness: "Cognitive spontaneity, physical spontaneity, social spontaneity, and manifest joy."[11] It is this last domain that we want to discuss: manifest joy. Before joy is attainable in the Christian life, some questions must be answered positively: Are my personal values constructive and realistic? How meaningful does my life seem? Are my beliefs and values helpful? Do I have a usable set of morals, standards, and ethics? Do I have a provision for the unknown? This latter is my spiritual scale to determine my ability to have manifest joy.

Yessick feels, and I agree, that there is a direct correlation between playfulness and spiritual health. You cannot be completely spiritually healthy with an absence of spontaneous playfulness. William Barclay developed an entire treatise on "The Humor of Christ." Jesus had fun. He had serious business to attend to, but He also had fun. He used puns, satire, hyperbole, and litotes. These figures of speech suggest playfulness.

Compassion fatigue can be diminished with playfulness that has no express purpose. Empty the garbage, and you can be free to celebrate. Find the disconnect activity and participate in it, and you will be free to celebrate. Have fun in the celebration, and it will be contagious.

Celebration Is Other Dimensional

I hesitated to connect with this idea. Charismatic behavior as we commonly see it on television and in some churches causes me some concern, and perhaps some envy. I do not fully and totally connect with some charismatic behavior characterized by speaking in tongues, sounds of ecstasy, uncontrolled noises and movements, bodies laid out on the floor. I do not diminish their right, that is, the right of those who participate. I just do not totally connect.

However, I do believe they experience a sense of celebration in which there is another dimension of feeling and expression. I still get goose bumps when I listen to the video of R. G. Lee's sermon, "Payday Someday." I cry when I watch Billy Graham extend an invitation in one of his crusades. The movie *Hoosiers,* a story about a country high school that won the state basketball tournament in Indiana, brings a lump to my throat. It reminds me of past fleeting moments of glory at Holcomb, Missouri, High School because the time frame was exactly the same, 1952–53.

Stories of unselfishness take me to a different plane. When Oscar Robinson, one of my childhood heroes, gave a kidney to a daughter, it was a model of love. That is celebration. What a legacy that must be. What a heritage to leave that must be.

On *20/20,* the story of a pug dog's surgical procedure which gave a spinal chord to a young child was other dimensional because of the sheer joy of the creative genius of a surgeon. The cameras covered the first meeting of the boy and the dog. I dare you not to cry. It was wonderful.

A love song sung in duet by Celine Dion and Luciano Pavoratti has been worn out on my CD. It still moves me. It is other dimensional.

Handel's *Messiah* causes me great exhilaration. The choral arrangement of "For unto us a Child is born, unto us a Son is given, and the government shall be upon His shoulders: and His name shall be called Wonderful, Counselor, the Mighty God, the Everlasting Father, the Prince of Peace" (from Isa. 9:6) is majestic, inspiring, and thrilling.[12] And the tradition of standing during the "Hallelujah" chorus of the work will move even the most exaggerated of musical illiterates.

These are special moments, moments when professionals extend their prowess in an extraordinary moment. The Christian faith is other dimensional. The expression of the Christian faith is other dimensional in the subtleties of everyday experience.

It can be seen best in a "thank you" that is unexpected. It can be seen in a simple "You are very special to me." "I love you because you are so kind" was a statement one pastor's wife shared with me about an unexpected response from her husband.

A friend was chairman of a community landscaping project. A decision the committee made about the placement of trees upset a neighbor. "You people think you run the world," he said.

"I'm sorry you are upset, but this was a community decision, and we feel it is best. Why don't you come over, and let's talk about some of the benefits."

My friend's wife waited for the end of the conversation. She said, "You have the most soothing voice when people are upset." They had been married 42 years. He told the story as a celebration of her affirmation. It was unexpected and wonderful to him.

Other-dimensional celebration events take place when people do unselfish things or say unselfish things. "I was wrong." "You are right" "You look great" "That was a nice thing for you to say" "Can I use that in a sermon?" "Will you give me permission to include that in my book?"

Wayne Oates took notes. That was a thrill. He was my guru, my mentor, and he really listened to what I had to say. I was overwhelmed with emotion. It was other dimensional. It was better than a Caribbean cruise. It was lasting. It was a celebration.

If he were still alive, Bear Bryant would appreciate this accolade of other-dimensional response: "If I coach next year, I pass Bear Bryant in the number of games coached. I don't want to do that. I'm not in Bear Bryant's class," said University of Iowa's "winningest football coach," Hayden Fry, who retired after 20 seasons, referring to the University of Alabama's legendary coach.[12]

Someday we may be able to celebrate death as we have celebrated life. I am uncomfortable with sensationalized euthanasia. I don't believe we should do God's work. But we do need to take the sting out of death. We need to feel the joy that Paul talked about in death. I was close to death just last year. Only in reflection do I realize just how close I was: A bleeding ulcer almost took my life. Then quadruple by-pass surgery 10 days later. Then kidney stones, and two months later, surgery to remove my gall bladder. The children in *Annie,* the musical, sang, "It's a Hard-Knock Life." Yeah, right. I wrestled with my mortality. I will again.

I discovered that I was not nearly as fearful as I expected. I must have listened to a few of my encouraging words about eternal life. The reality of seeing my parents and friends again was exciting. The idea of being with Christ in glory was no longer a sermon illustration. It was, in a sense, a real celebration. But in those moments when I think again, *Is this it?* I am fearful but not mortified. I think this could be the beginning of something new, something really exciting. This could be the beginning of all those things that I studied but have not experienced. This could be the best part of life: dying. The unknown is the only disturbing factor. The hope of glory is triumphant. This is truly other dimensional. Death is the ultimate celebration.

At First Baptist Church, Nashville, a marvelous choir sang the "Hallelujah" chorus at the memorial service for Elgene Phillips, a minister at the Sunday School Board (now LifeWay Christian Resources of the Southern Baptist Convention). More than two decades have passed since then, but it remains a highlight of celebration in my mind. It was other dimensional. It took us to the realm of the other world and into the presence of God.

"I've Been to the Bottom and It's Solid"

Tommy Cunningham gave me permission to use his story. It is a story of despair—but then celebration. It is a story of no hope—and, then, hope.

December 2, 1998, our conversation was brief but heavy.

"Good morning, Tommy. This is Brooks Faulkner with LeaderCare."

"Good morning, Brooks."

"I just read your story, and I want you to know how deeply I was touched. I also wanted you to know that we are concerned with your well-being."

"Thank you. I do feel I am on the way back up."

"Please know that I am not meddling, just concerned."

"You already know that in January 1997, I was terminated from a church that I had pastored for six years. I felt battered and confused. Seething within me was an indignation for all those I perceived were involved in my termination.

"But the crowning blow came when I was asked to leave an adjunct teaching position at a nearby seminary. I had taken great pride in pouring my life into the lives of young preacher boys.

This termination came only weeks after the church vote. I was told it would be best if I would left the classroom immediately.

"I started pastoring a new church, but my anger was like a cancer spreading into every room of my heart. My questions of 'Why, Lord?' rang out from my heart like the cry of a wounded soldier. Bitterness soon found fertile soil in my grieving heart. I became a spiritual hermit, finding protection within the four walls of my new church office. Prayer was absent from my study and my life. I was mad at God, disillusioned with people, and determined to show the world I could survive. I became so empty. My life was a wasteland of human failure.

"On October 30, 1998, after returning home from a high-school football game and retiring, there came a compelling desire to talk to my closest friend. Driven by fear and panic, I dialed the number. There was no answer. An answering machine began its prerecorded message, and I found myself shouting to the response mode, 'Please pick up, please, for God's sake answer!' I must have tried half a dozen times to reach my friend with the same result. My desperation had reached its limit; the devil had done his work.

"With a knife in plain sight, I slashed my left wrist. Blood began immediately to drop to the floor. I wanted to die. Truly, I was shackled by a heavy burden. It took six policemen to carry me to a local hospital. I remember nothing of that evening other than what I have been told. I fought against my helpers, requiring handcuffs to restrain my arms. They even had to use pepper spray to overcome me. All the while I am reported to be screaming, 'No one loves me!' The ambulance took me to a large hospital where eventually I became a patient of a Christian doctor."

"It may sound empty, but God still loves you," I said.

"I know," he says, "And I'm on the way up. I have been to the bottom, and it is solid. People have been wonderful. My wife has been there for me. My family and friends have supported me. They saw me at the lowest, and they loved me anyway." He stopped. We waited. And waited. We hurt together. A prayerful spirit that is too often trivialized was apparent and evident with us both.

"What have I learned?" he asked. "I'm learning to trust Jesus and to stand still and see the deliverance of the Lord. The Word of God has become powerful. I see a greater need for Jesus to be first in my life everyday. Listening to the Spirit calms my heart. The Psalms have been comforting. I'm beginning to receive grace as a gift, not something I have to earn."

"What activities are helpful to you?" I asked.

"My wife and I are praying together twice a day. I am walking six miles a day and disconnecting with everything but God. I am remembering that God loves me and with a pure love that I don't have to work for. And it endures. I have truly been to the bottom, and I am on the way up."

"Emil Turner, the executive director, Arkansas Baptist State Convention, shared this with me because you gave him permission. I know he will continue to pray for you as will we at LeaderCare and Jimmy Draper, our president at LifeWay Christian Resources."

"You can't know what this means to me."

Celebration is knowing you are on the way back. It feels good to know that you have been to the bottom and it is solid.

---

[1] See Rudyard Kipling, "If," stanza 2.

[2] Charles Figley, *Compassion Fatigue* (Bristol, PA: Brunner/Mazel, 1995), 12.

[3] Ibid., 165.

[4] Ibid.

[5] Ibid., 166.

[6] Ibid.

[7] Ibid.

[8] Ibid., 167.

[9] Ibid.

[10] Tommy Yessick, "The Relationship Between Leisure Disposition and Total Well Being in Middle Aged Adults," Ph.D. dissertation, University of Utah, 1990. An additional work that is useful in this area of celebration is Patricia Farrell and Herberta M. Lundegren, *The Process of Recreation Programming Theory and Technique,* 2nd edition (New York: Macmillan Publishing Co., 1983).

[11] Yessick, 56.

[12] G. F. Handel, *The Messiah*, part 1, chorus 12.

[13] *Newsweek*, 7 December 1998.

WAITING—IT AIN'T OVER 'TIL IT'S OVER

1	You can't fix people; only God can.
2	You don't have to expand your word output to be convincing.
3	We need to spend more time with the weak and those who can't do anything for us. Jesus did.
4	God doesn't need us, but He does love us.
5	It is not the renegades who do you in but the Pharisees.
6	To receive a blessing, you have to give one.
7	Legacies aren't what they are trumped up to be.
8	Treat church members like friends not church members.
9	Getting your way may win the battle but ultimately lose the war.
10	There is a time to stand up for what is right.
11	"Aha's" don't teach you as much as the "Oh, my's."
12	Scolding is rarely helpful but always memorable.
13	If you bail out in ministry, you may cut your chances of busting out in ministry.
14	A quick fix is not always long-term healing.
15	Anger is a killer.
16	Never get in so big a hurry that you don't have fun.
17	Criticism in ministry is inevitable and sometimes painful but rarely terminal.
18	You have a choice in life, but God is going to love you anyway.

Chapter 10: It Ain't Over 'til It's Over

"Keep yourselves in God's love as you wait for the mercy of our Lord Jesus Christ to bring you to eternal life" (Jude 21).

The message of Jude was a call to persevere. So is our call. We have a call from God. It is to persevere during the bad times but also during the good times. During the bad times, the perseverance is a demand for keeping spirits up. During the good times, the call to persevere is keeping spirits in perspective. The latter will avoid the trivial pursuit of glamour. We know it does not exist. But we do represent God. And that is the "good times" of glory.

Jimmy Connors once said, "Experience is a great advantage. The problem is that when you get the experience, you're too old to do anything about it."[1] Many ministers feel that way. I have been working in the area of church administration and with pastors and staff as an audience for the last 35 years. During that time, I have heard these words hundreds of times: "I wish I had heard that during my seminary training. I believe it would have saved me a lot of grief." It might have. But probably not. Experience comes, unfortunately, as a result of adversity. It teaches us. But our resistance to change and reluctance to learn delay application. The result is that we may ultimately learn but regret that we did not learn the lesson earlier.

Yogi Berra probably said it first: "It ain't over 'til it's over." But ministers can say it as well. The sad part of the story is that many churches feel it is over before it is over. We know we still have many gifts and missions to fulfill, but churches have an unwritten time log that says ministers are less productive after age 55 (or some other arbitrary number). Finding fulfillment and a productive manner of service in the latter stages of ministry is, to many, an enigma. To others it is fantasy.

In considering career issues in ministry, we have formed the following alliterative design for ages:

Start-up in Ministry—Ages 15–25
- Vocational dreams
- The call to ministry
- Assuming a general role as minister
- Discovering gifts and skills for ministry
- Educational preparation

Stabilization—Ages 25–35
- Advanced educational preparation
- Examining the dream
- A call to a specific church or ministry position
- Fine-tuning gifts and skills in ministry
- Finding support systems and mentoring networks

Summit—Ages 35–60
- Assuming preferred role in ministry
- Call to preferred place or position
- Testing the dreams
- Adjusting the gifts and skills in ministry
- Ultimate legacy in becoming God's purposive agent

Simplification—Age 60 and over
- Handing on the dream
- Finding comfort zones
- Less-public roles in ministry
- Support drawn from younger persons
- Reentry into ministry areas suited to age and energy

The phrase, "It ain't over 'til it's over," suggests simplification. Many have said, "I will never retire." Agencies and institutions have other ideas. So do many churches. Most ministers have common sense in knowing when to begin the process of "winding down." Retirement is not preparation to die. Retirement can mean adjusting the quality of ministry according to age and energy. A part of life is adjustment. The skillful and compassionate minister will know what he is able to do, and adjust accordingly. One retired minister told me, "I am just waiting to see what God is going to do with me next. It has never been more exciting."

In 1988, the Sunday School Board released a book entitled *The Holy Spirit in the Minister's Life Changes.* We asked Herschel Hobbs, the venerable "patron saint" of Southern Baptists, to write the chapter on retirement. When we talked about the title with him, he said, "Why don't you just call it, 'Next Stop, Glory.'" He is now in glory. But he left a remarkable legacy, and much of it was given after his seventieth year. He wrote in his opening statement: "My seminary classmates often heard John R. Sampey say, 'As an apple grows old, it either mellows or rots. I hope to mellow.' His words meant something to me then. They mean much more now."[2]

Dr. Hobbs continued: "Personally, I never have liked the word *retirement*. I prefer *retreadment*. When you retire from a stated ministry, you should retread for a different type of ministry."[3]

My own brother, J. D., is 80. He owns McCaul Tire and Appliance Story in Kennett, Missouri. Recently, when I mentioned retirement after he had had a bout with an aneurism, he said, "I don't want to retire. Too many of my friends have retired, and quit. Too soon, they died." J. D. still works a full day. He is still responsible for a multimillion-dollar business and manages it well. He may have retreaded (as he does his tires) several times, but he still runs a lucrative business.

Ministry is full of opportunities. Winning people to Christ is never over. Work with Christian discipleship and equipping others is a never-ending story. Stepping back and allowing others to do the heavy work is full of fulfillment. You no longer need to "prove yourself." You have done much of your work. Your legacy has been established. There is always a Joshua for a Moses to continue the work of ministry. But it ain't over 'til it's over.

Some of the lessons learned that help us know that it ain't over 'til it's over are:

We have renounced "fixing" as a way of life.—Ministers cannot fix people. Only God can do that.

We have an inside joke about "fixing" people in LeaderCare. It is amusing because it is incredible. We cannot fix people. We can care, pray with them, listen. But we cannot fix them.

We have downsized our word output.—We have learned that opinions are much more powerful if we keep them to ourselves. An opportunity will occur; and we will not have to fabricate, legislate, or manipulate our opinion. We know it ain't over 'til it's over.

We have learned to spend more time with the unnoticed, the weak, the helpless.—We now remember that it is the meek who will inherit the earth, not the megachurch pastors, or heads of agencies, or presidents of conventions, or even moderators of associations. Big bucks, big connections, big numbers, big denominational positions are nice accolades. But the real glue is the time we spend with persons who cannot help us but we can be a minister to them. Was this what Jesus had in mind when He said, "The first shall be last, and the last shall be first"? (see Matt. 19:30).

We have learned that God does not need us.—He just loves us. He could do His work without us. He chooses to allow us to do His kingdom work. It is a blessing not an assignment. It is a privilege not a responsibility. We should feel His grace. Too often I have allowed myself to feel guilt when I should be feeling gentleness.

We have learned that it is not the renegades and curmudgeons in churches that do us in; it is the Pharisees.—I have frequently been reminded of a profound statement about Pharisaism: "The meanest man I ever saw always stayed within the law."

Jesus had trouble with the Pharisees. Most ministers do. It is not the sinners who do us in; it is the saints—perhaps jaded saints.

We have learned that if you want to receive a blessing from God and others, you must be a blessing to others.—The best teams in basketball are those with players who don't care who gets the credit. The best lesson in life is to be a blessing without expecting a blessing from others. It is serendipitous. It comes automatically. It is unexpected. It is undeserved. Justice is blind. God does not have scales. He just blesses. He does not weigh what has been done and then try to measure things out. He just gives freely of His grace. That is how blessing works. Be a blessing, and sooner or later you will receive a blessing.

We have learned that a legacy is probably laughable.— Kindness, on the other hand, lasts forever. "What do you want said about you when you are gone?" As I have thought about it, who cares? A legacy is not as important as doing what God expects while we are still here: Be kind to one another. That is what Jesus did.

A murderer, standing before the firing squad, was asked if he had any final requests. He said, "Why, yes—a bulletproof vest." When a prominent physician was asked what he wanted said about him in his obituary, he answered, "I would like them to print a retraction because it was a mistake and the guy is still breathing."

We make far too much of death. We preach and teach the biblical truths of eternity and then pretend death is a monster. Death is painful and scary because it means facing the unknown. But we also know that death will take us to be with our Lord. That, in itself, is reassuring. I would like my legacy to be, "He was born again, and he has gone to be with the Lord." Until then, I would like to learn more about how to be kind to people, even those I don't like. And that's hard.

We have learned to treat church members like friends, not like church members.—You can "pastor" people without "patronizing" people. It is not easy. Some church members make heavy demands. But if you treat them as responsible adults, it can happen. If you practice the principle of the priesthood of every believer, you will help them to deal with their own problems. You can love them without rescuing them. You can support them without fixing them. Church members should be treated as friends.

We have learned that getting your way at the expense of someone losing diminishes your stock significantly.—The ideal solution in Baptist life is to have everyone feel they have won. The most difficult aspect of skills in ministry is to affirm the humanity of those with whom you work—both staff members and church members. As I write, billions of dollars are being lost in the National Basketball Association because people want to win at the expense of others. Both players and owners are losing. It's OK to eat crow now and then. Paul Powell suggested he had eaten it fried, boiled, broiled, and raw. "It doesn't taste good in any form." But it does have a way of diminishing the negative returns. It is not bad to lose if those whom you care about are winning. Selflessness may be a lost art. But it is one of the best ways of showing the spirit of Christ.

But we have learned that neither should we become an emotional dump site.—There is a time to stand for what is right. Ministers must live by a moral code, and they should help people understand they are loyal to this code. It should be based on biblical mandates. To continue to permit neurotic persons to dump on you without standing up for yourself will erode your credibility.

Perhaps one way is to adapt the adage, "Speak softly and carry a big stick," into, "Stand firmly when others swing an unmerciful verbal stick." You can be kind without being a patsy. You can give in without giving up. You can be caring and loving without being dumped on by insensitive Pharisees.

James Thurber once wrote these words, "You might as well fall flat on your face as lean over too far backward." [4]

We have learned that more has been accomplished in ministry from the "Oh, my's" than from the "aha's."—Adversity challenges the mind. That is the "oh, my!" Discovery touches the heart. That is the "aha!" Both are earthshaking. But "aha's" are too often short-lived. "Oh, my's" have long-lasting effects.

We have learned that scolding others is rarely helpful, and it's almost completely memorable.—We know that feedback is helpful. Criticism, even constructive criticism, puts a dent in relationships. Jesus did not like the lifestyle of the rich young ruler. He was straight with him. But Jesus allowed the rich young ruler to discover his own deficiencies. He did not have to point them out to him. Jesus loved him. The difference between feedback and criticism is that those who give us feedback care about us. Those who criticize us are attempting to "put us down."

We have learned that there are alternatives to bailing out.—Options include sabbaticals, leaves of absence, therapy, and support groups. Find ways to change a boring routine into an exciting ministry. A minister does not have to bail out. It ain't over 'til it's over.

We have learned that there is a difference between a quick fix and long-term healing.—Some just need a little encouragement. This is a Band-Aid™. It is a quick fix. Motivational experts are excellent at this formula. "Make a list. Find out what is good. Forget the bad. Everything will be all right." It works for a few. But it is woefully deficient for those in real need. It borders on "shallow theology."

Redemption is painful. It is the difference between surgery and an aspirin. Redemption means taking the old life and re-working it. God works in mysterious ways. It is not all peaches and cream. It is frequently a long, arduous process of cleansing. God's grace is sufficient, but it is not always lightning quick. All healing is divine, but not all healing is quick.

Physiological pain can increase spiritual pain. Guilt can be long lasting if the chemical imbalance in the body creates a depression that feels incurable.

A husband who had lived with his wife for 45 years, 20 of them heavy with manic-depression in her life, was asked how he maintained his equilibrium and still focused on the grace of God. He said: "I have always known I was in this for the long haul. God has always had something better planned. I may not understand it, but I believe it." It will never be a quick fix. It will always be laden with antidepressants, sleeping aids, and other related medications; but with the help of the sustaining power of God's grace, and the long haul of "love at all costs," it is manageable.

We have learned that anger is a killer.—It depletes. It destroys relationships. It leads to long-term resentment, bitterness, and cynicism. It is nonproductive. Also, it is a serious sin. The Bible clearly tells us to be angry and sin not. It means we cannot help the angry feelings. We can certainly choose not to hold on to them.

In a recent issue of *Leadership,* Ben Patterson and Zig Ziglar were being interviewed on the subject of "joy in ministry." "I've got a Ph.D. in anger," said Patterson. "On both sides of my family, never an angry thought is left unexpressed, and we're all pugilists. When in seminary, I went into counseling because I was so angry. But I became only more angry, because therapy told me I had a right to be angry." The solution, he suggested, was repentance. "We simply cannot be grateful and angry, or joyful and angry."[5] We must repent, and stop being angry with God's help.

Ziglar added, "I often tell my audience, 'Now this won't get you out of clinical depression, but if you're down in the dumps or upset, the first thing to do is write down what you're upset about. Second, ask yourself, "How long do I want to stay there?"

"'Third, put a deadline on your being down in the dumps, like maybe until three o'clock this afternoon.'"[6]

You may not be able to turn off the churning feelings of anger inside, but you have the freedom of choice in expression. You do not have to express everything you feel. The damaging parts of ministry come not in feeling but in expressions. Be angry and sin not.

We have learned that you should not to get in too big a hurry to have fun in ministry.—It's time to learn another way to live. We must put the joy back into ministry. Life is too short to waste it on hurry.

John Ortberg tells a wonderful story: "A newspaper in Tacoma, Washington, carried the story of Tattoo, the basset hound. Tattoo didn't intend to go for an evening run, but when his owner shut his leash in the car door and took off for a drive with Tattoo still outside the vehicle, he had no choice.

"Motorcycle officer Terry Filbert noticed a passing vehicle with something dragging behind it. 'The basset hound was picking them up and putting them down as fast as he could.' He chased the car to a stop, and Tattoo was rescued, but not before the dog had reached a speed of 20–25 miles per hour, rolling over several times."[7]

If you live like Tattoo, you can't enjoy ministry. Every day will be marked by picking them up and putting them down as fast as you can. You can bet your bottom dollar you are going to roll over several times. If you want joy, you must eliminate hurry from your life. And don't get your leash caught in your church's activity door.

We have learned that criticism is inevitable and painful but not terminal.—It just feels like it—terminal, that is.

On ESPN, former NHL goalie Jacques Plante was asked how he liked his position. He said, "How would you like a job where, if you made a mistake, a big red light goes on and 18,000 people boo?"

"It's a hard-knock life." But you're in it for the long haul. You are probably going to outlast them anyway. The spastic critics are usually prone to get bored and leave your church. Be patient.

If the criticism is legitimate, then learn from it. If not, live with it. My physician told me, "Three out of three people die. So shut up and deal." He had a warped sense of humor. I loved it.

We have learned that you can play the victim, the rescuer, or the survivor.—If you play the victim, it is short lived, and pity soothes few hurts. If you play the rescuer, people will love you, but their need will suffocate you. If you play the survivor, you will wait on the providence of God, but you will wait expectantly and hopefully. God has something better planned than we could imagine. "The Lord longs to be gracious to you; he rises to show you compassion. For the Lord is a God of justice. Blessed are all who wait for him!" (Isa. 30:18).

You may not get the church you hoped for. God has something better planned for you. You may not get the committee or trustee position you wished for. God has something better planned for you. You may not get the plush denominational position you were promised. (It doesn't exist anyway.) God has something better planned for you.

Wait on the Lord. Trust His providence. He will not forsake you. He will not forget you. The desperation of loneliness and isolation may prove to be overpowering, but wait on Him. He is still there. He still loves you.

It ain't over 'til it's over.

---

[1] Jimmy Connors, as quoted in *The Communicator*, October 1998: 5.

[2] Herschel Hobbs, "The Holy Spirit and Retirement in Minister (Age Seventy and Up)," *The Holy Spirit in the Minister's Life Changes* (Nashville: Convention, 1988), 99.

[3] Ibid., 104.

[4] James Thurber, as quoted in *The Communicator*, August, 1998: 2.

[5] An Interview with Ben Patterson and Zig Ziglar, *Leadership*, Fall 1998: 27.

[6] Ibid.

[7] Ibid., 34.

POSTSCRIPT

We asked some pastors and other leaders in the Southern Baptist Convention to tell us who inspired them. They were generous in helping us put this postscript together.

One pastor said: "I look for the following in those I admire: Is he balanced? Would I like to have him for my pastor? Is he faithful to Scripture? Do I respect him even if I differ with him? Does he still have joy in what he is doing? Is he a personal witness? What is the character and quality of his relationship with his wife and children? Does he still make personal pastoral calls?" That is not a bad description of a great role model for us preacher types.

Faithful, responsible, and *caring* were said of Robert Naylor, John Newport, C. W. Brister, John Bisagno, and Jimmy Draper. *Vision, courage,* and *integrity* were words used often about Landrum Leavell, Charles Carter, Jim Henry, and Paul Powell. Ernest Mosley was described as seeing ways to grant new beginnings.

Bob Dale wrote about Claude McFerron, "He literally loved me into the kingdom of God." Leonard Dupree wrote about J. Robert White, "His leadership is highly challenging but at the same time highly trusting." Rick Lance described Jim Henry as "a tremendous pastor who values people and loves the work." Roy Edgemon, wrote of Charles Roselle, a "pastor who has created the model of church ministry for the 21st century."

Laney Johnson was described as "a consistent, faithful, soul-winning pastor of the same church for 38 years; also strong in staff development." Selah for any pastor who can stay, survive, and serve for 38 years. He helps the average for all of us.

About Robert Jeffress: "Brilliant expositor of Scripture, exciting writer, and a warm, loving pastor."

Tom Elliff wrote of "Preacher" Hallock, "'Preacher' taught me the importance of spending time in the Word of God every day." He also wrote, "Dr. R. G. Witty, at age 92, taught me that life is not over until it's over. He is still a prolific writer, frequent speaker, effective consultant."

Wendell Estep shared, "Dr. Adrian Rogers is a model of integrity." "Warren Hultgren had the respect and ear of his city." And, "Charles Fuller has invested his life into the church he has served from his younger days."

Ronnie Floyd said of Jimmy Draper, "He is a great role model for me because of his commitment to people and his continued interest in their personal lives." "Adrian Rogers is a role model because of his courageous stand for morality and righteousness in this nation." And, "John Maxwell because of his passion to invest his life in leadership all across the world."

Freddie Gage gave a role call of faith for the men who have become his role models: J. Harold Smith, W. A. Criswell, C. E. Autrey, James T. Draper, and Billy Graham.

Robert Haskins wrote, "Clyde Steelman Jr. is so patient with people. He is positive about and with people."

Larry Chapman, Charles Graves, Mark Hartman, and Russell Duck were named as persons who encourage young preachers.

Rex Horne named Wendell Estep as one who "modeled the meaning of friendship."

Johnny Hunt said Fred Wolfe "prayed for me regularly," and of Adrian Rogers, "He made me feel important."

Dick Maples served several churches as pastor and is now a denominational leader in Texas. He served under William Henry Crouch and Elwin L. Skiles as youth minister. They used their leadership to demonstrate pastoral caring. He learned well.

Louis McBurney said Carlisle Marney "colored outside the lines and affirmed our calling to Marble Retreat." Ed Bratcher and Fred Smith helped him solidify his commitment to Jesus. Charles

Wellborn challenged his intellectual commitment to Christianity.

Reginald McDonough was influenced by Charles Fuller, Neal Jones, and Ralph McIntyre. He wrote of Howard Foshee, "He was a grower of people."

Two persons who influenced David Meacham's life were Michael Rochelle and Joe Taylor. Both had a "sense of humor and a love for people." Scott Williamson, Hoyt Savage, and Robb Zinn were influencers because of their zeal for evangelism.

James Merritt was influenced by Adrian Rogers, Jerry Vines, John Macarthur, and Warren Wiersbe. Jerry Vines "took time to be a personal friend." Troy Morrison was influenced by Charles Carter, Richard Trader, and Earl Potts. Earl Potts was "warm, friendly, courteous, and genteel in his Christlike demeanor, and this caused him to be loved by all who knew him."

Bill Pinson named role models Walter Bartels, James Harris, James Landes, L. B. Reavis, and Bo Baker. Bo Baker "combined evangelistic zeal, pastoral concern, and inspiring worship linked with carefully prepared, solidly biblical sermons."

Jack Riddlehoover named Tim Owens, Stan Alcorn, Randy White, Chad Selph, and John Hall, "strong preachers, sharp minds, and pastoral spirits."

Mike Rochelle named Frank Lewis, John Mark Simmons, Rob Zinn, and Rick Warren. Of Frank Lewis, he wrote, "ability to present the Word with clarity, practicality, and brevity."

Some of Adrian Rogers' role models include Stephen Olford, Jerry Vines, Ed Young, James Dobson, and Tom Elliff. He said of Olford and Vines, "gifted exposition of the Word of God and fearless preaching." Of Ed Young: "innovative leadership and ability to think big." Of Tom Elliff: "sincerity and prayer power."

Cecil Seagle named Jim Henry, James Goodson, John Sullivan, and yours truly (thank you, Cecil). Of Sullivan, he said, "friend and preacher of exceptional insight and passion."

Anthony Jordan named Rick Warren: "Purpose-driven approach to reaching people for Christ."

Jimmy Sheffield named D. L. Lowrie, Doug Dillard, Cary Heard, and Frank Pollard (whom he called "one of the greatest communicators I've ever heard").

Joe Stacker named Harold Stephens, Calvin Miller, Bill Harbin, and James Barry, a former preaching consultant and a member of Joe's church who "challenges me to sharpen my preaching skills every Sunday."

John Sullivan was inspired by W. A. Criswell, Huber Drumwright, Robert Naylor, and A. L. Smith, who "knew his church members by name."

Dan Yeary was described as "the most compassionate person I know" by Bill Taylor.

Gordon Clinard was described as "the most excellent preacher I ever heard" by Joe Trull.

Jimmy Allen balanced his ethics and evangelism, according to Trull.

"Gary Watkins spent time training me for ministry rather than just telling me to minister," said Emil Turner.

Dan Yeary was touched by the "authentic grace and loving communication" of Buckner Fanning. Ken Chafin had "down-to-earth application of his Christianity."

Role models in ministry are caring persons. They know how to communicate the gospel of Christ, and they have patterned their lives after leading others to Him. They like people. They love people. They take time for others and have courage and wisdom during adversity. They have no need to impress others but give themselves generously and willingly to the weak, helpless, hungry, thirsty, and growing persons in the world. They are family-type persons. They may not have perfect families, but they count their families as the most sacred institution, even before their church. They do not neglect their church but give themselves to making the church the extension of the incarnation of

Christ. They are balanced in their theology, ethics, and value systems so that it does not rob them of the vitality of ministry. Then they are free to GET ON TOP OF THEIR WORK!

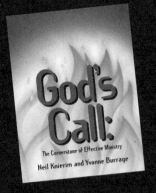